# CHARACTER BUILDING

*The*
## ABCs
*of* Building Depth
*and* Strength *of* Character

*Jim Boeglin*

Copyright © 2018 Jim Boeglin.

All rights reserved. No part of this book may be used or reproduced by any means, graphic, electronic, or mechanical, including photocopying, recording, taping or by any information storage retrieval system without the written permission of the author except in the case of brief quotations embodied in critical articles and reviews.

This book is a work of non-fiction. Unless otherwise noted, the author and the publisher make no explicit guarantees as to the accuracy of the information contained in this book and in some cases, names of people and places have been altered to protect their privacy.

Archway Publishing books may be ordered through booksellers or by contacting:

Archway Publishing
1663 Liberty Drive
Bloomington, IN 47403
www.archwaypublishing.com
1 (888) 242-5904

Because of the dynamic nature of the Internet, any web addresses or links contained in this book may have changed since publication and may no longer be valid. The views expressed in this work are solely those of the author and do not necessarily reflect the views of the publisher, and the publisher hereby disclaims any responsibility for them.

Any people depicted in stock imagery provided by Getty Images are models, and such images are being used for illustrative purposes only. Certain stock imagery © Getty Images.

ISBN: 978-1-4808-6213-5 (sc)
ISBN: 978-1-4808-6212-8 (hc)
ISBN: 978-1-4808-6214-2 (e)

Library of Congress Control Number: 2018905384

Print information available on the last page.

Archway Publishing rev. date: 05/03/2018

The word *character* is one of those versatile English words with multiple meanings. We sometimes refer to a person as a "character," when we mean that he or she is different, unique, interesting, lovable, funny, colorful, amusing, entertaining, eccentric, bizarre, or even weird. Characters are often memorable. It may or may not be a compliment to call someone a character. And then there are "devious characters," who manipulate the system, lie, cheat, and seem to willingly do anything to get what they want. These particular characters are not the subject of this book. "Shady characters" operate on the fringes of legality and are generally not trusted or respected. Devious and shady characters are the antithesis of what it means to have character.

This book is about an entirely different meaning of character. This character has an intangible quality not readily visible to the naked eye, but we usually know when we are in its presence. When we refer to a person as "having character," it is said in admiration of that person's essential qualities of personality, inner strength, temperament, and makeup.

People of character have a moral compass that points true north. They are honest, trustworthy, dependable, steadfast, strong, and committed to doing the right thing. Other people look up to them and respect them. These characters have a positive impact on the lives of those around them, and we rely on them for leadership. They have personality *characteristics* that other people value. Having character is an absolute necessity for a life well lived.

Some characters I have known have also had character. Those two meanings are not mutually exclusive. In my experience, it is an excellent combination for a person to possess: funny, interesting, unique, and lovable, as well as honest, strong, and dependable.

History has provided us with role models possessing strong, deep character. People like George Washington, John Adams, Abe Lincoln, Franklin D. Roosevelt, Winston Churchill, Margaret Thatcher, Dr. Martin Luther King Jr., Mother Teresa, and Gandhi have demonstrated their depth and strength of character on the world stage. The world is a better place for their having been here. Character never goes out of style. The world of the twenty-first century could use more persons of character, both in political and business leadership positions and in the trenches of everyday life.

Character is the sum total of our personalities. It is made up of many building blocks, some of which are explored in this book. A few people seem to have an innate sense of character that is genetic. They appear to have been born with it. For most people, however, character is an acquired trait. It is the result of a continuing effort to do the right thing, choosing thoughts and actions that are strong, confident, brave, kind, loving, helpful, and positive. According to James Allen, author of *As a Man Thinketh*, our character is not a thing of chance. Rather, it is the sum of all our thoughts. We are free to choose our thoughts and thereby mold our character.

I think of character as an individual bank account. We make deposits to our character account when we choose to be kind, honest, helpful, tough in the face of adversity, or committed to doing the right thing. We make withdrawals from the account when we choose to be negative, fearful, less than honest, or hurtful to ourselves or someone else. Every one of us determines, consciously or unconsciously, the current balance in our character account. A character account is infinitely more important than a bank account.

Character can be learned as a result of life's tests and challenges. The aging process is often a helpful ingredient in developing character. It is relatively rare to meet a teenager or young adult with a fully developed sense of character. It is a more common trait among the adult and mature populations. It can take decades of living to build character.

Many young adults learn about character while serving in the military, where toughness, dedication, discipline, and commitment are the curriculum. For them, lessons learned in military service can be the launching pad for living a life of character. Tom Brokaw referred to the veterans of WWII as the "greatest generation" because so many returning servicemen and servicewomen acquired character as the result of their wartime experiences and applied it to their postwar lives.

For others, character is learned from grandparents, parents, teachers, mentors, religious leaders, spouses, children, grandchildren, or associates. Sometimes it is acquired as a result of difficult personal challenges.

This book is dedicated to all the persons of character in the world, past and present, whether or not they are characters. You may be one of them, or you may be a work in process. I have lived among many people of character during my lifetime, and while names have been changed and circumstances modified, a few of them are mentioned in this book.

If I do not have character, it is my own damn fault because I have certainly been given ample opportunities in the past three-quarters of a century to learn it from the people and the circumstances in my life.

# CONTENTS

Acknowledgments ................................................................. xi
Introduction ...................................................................... xiii

| | | |
|---|---|---|
| A | Attitude | 1 |
| B | Being | 10 |
| C | Confidence | 15 |
| D | Defenselessness | 23 |
| E | Ethical Behavior | 29 |
| F | Forgiveness | 34 |
| G | Gratitude | 42 |
| H | Humor | 48 |
| I | Integrity | 54 |
| J | Justice | 59 |
| K | Kindness | 63 |
| L | Love | 67 |
| M | Mission | 73 |
| N | Neighbors | 79 |
| O | Outside the Box | 84 |
| P | Peaceful | 89 |
| Q | Quiet Mind | 95 |
| R | Real | 98 |
| S | Strength | 103 |
| T | Trust | 108 |
| U | Understanding | 113 |

| V | Values | 118 |
| W | Wisdom | 122 |
| X | X-Ray Vision | 126 |
| Y | Yet | 129 |
| Z | Zero Fears | 132 |

Closing Thoughts ................................................................. 135
Powerful Affirmations For Character Building ................ 139
About the Author ................................................................. 141

# ACKNOWLEDGMENTS

The ability to read and write is one of the important measures of a society being considered a civilization. Mesopotamia developed the cuneiform script as a means of communicating in writing. Hieroglyphics were used in early civilizations and preceded the alphabet.

Most scholars agree that the modern alphabet has its origins in ancient Egypt, nearly five thousand years ago. From Egypt the alphabet was passed on to Phoenicia, where it began including vowels as well as consonants. From there it was spread to the Greeks, Etruscans, and Romans. Changes and improvements were made each time the alphabet was shared with another part of the civilized world, eventually evolving into our modern version. As with many worthwhile things in life, the alphabet was a cumulative effort with diverse contributors.

So we have thousands of years of civilization to thank for our ability to communicate in writing today. These civilizations came primarily from North Africa, the Middle East, and Southern Europe. Without their early contributions, we might not have books, newspapers, computers, or the internet.

I would not have been able to write this book without the benefit of the alphabet. In addition, I have used the alphabet as a form of structure for describing the building blocks of character. I am grateful to the scholars of earlier civilizations who helped to develop this important vehicle for communication.

# INTRODUCTION

I have not served in the military, and at my current age it is highly unlikely that I will have that experience in this lifetime. Student deferments, getting married, and fathering two children kept me one step ahead of the draft during the Vietnam War. By the time I graduated from law school, Uncle Sam was no longer interested in my service. That was okay with me. I would learn about character in nonmilitary ways.

The closest I came to military service was as a third grader. My teacher was a Benedictine nun, Sergeant Wilhelmina, a.k.a. Sister Wilhelmina. She was about four feet ten inches tall and couldn't have weighed ninety pounds, but Sister Wilhelmina packed a big punch in that tiny body. She was a tough, no-nonsense disciplinarian who would have made Bobby Knight look like a wimp. The truth is Sister Wilhelmina scared the crap out of me and my fellow third graders. Our knuckles, butts, and ears took a beating from her. I created the class motto, which was in the form of a question to our teacher: "Sister, will hell mean a worse place than this classroom?" Of course, the question was never verbalized directly to Sister Wilhelmina.

There was very little joy in that classroom, but we learned all about reading, writing, arithmetic, religion, guilt, fear, punishment, and discipline. Her approach was a significant factor in my becoming school spelling champ two years running. I was afraid of misspelling a word in her class.

From our perspective as grade-schoolers, Sister Wilhelmina was not an entertaining character we wanted to get to know and spend time with. In her own way, though, she had character. She truly cared about our education and was committed to teaching us. She was not someone we found amusing, but she was memorable. I doubt that any of my classmates have forgotten that nun. Our daily goal was to remain under the radar so she wouldn't pick us out of the crowd. We were in survival mode.

To make matters worse, Sister Wilhelmina was assigned to our class again in fourth grade and then again in fifth grade. It was the longest three years in any of our lives. Suicidal threats among my classmates may have been the reason the school board finally assigned a different nun for sixth grade. My memory is that Sister Wilhelmina was retired and turned out to pasture at the convent.

It was during the third grade that I became proficient in reciting the alphabet backward as well as forward. I could actually recite it faster in reverse, and I can still do it now, sixty-five years later. My early fascination with the alphabet, words, and reading led to my interest in writing.

The alphabet provides the building blocks for our words and language. Like the alphabet there are also universal building blocks that can help us to move our lives in the direction of our potential, toward a happier, healthier, more meaningful and fulfilling experience—a life of character. So, in a sense, this book is also dedicated to Sister Wilhelmina. From the perspective of looking back all these years later, I can almost appreciate her efforts to instill in me a sense of discipline.

My knuckles, butt, and ears have healed, and Sister Wilhelmina no longer scares the crap out of me. On a recent trip to my hometown of Ferdinand, Indiana, I climbed the hill to the Benedictine convent to say hello to a few of my favorite teaching nuns who were still alive. Before I left, I visited the nuns' cemetery and found the grave marker for Sister Wilhelmina. A part of me needed to make sure she was really gone. May she rest in peace.

## Trilogy

This book is the second in a series I have dubbed the Bike Writer Trilogy. To the best of my knowledge, intention, and belief, there will be a third book forthcoming.

Book 1, *The Bike Writer*, is a personal sharing of the paths I have taken and the lessons learned along the way. It recounts growing up the youngest of seven children in Ferdinand, a small town in Southern Indiana; recovering from an overdose of Catholicism as a child; raising a family; surviving an unplanned divorce; learning lessons from seventy years of biking in eleven different states in the United States and the Romantic Road in Germany; practicing law for more than three decades; being a Florida Realtor for a decade and a half; and being an active participant in the aging process.

Biking has been an important vehicle for me as I've traveled through life. It has been a source of physical exercise to stay fit, including rehabbing after triple bypass surgery, and a time to let my mind wander, questioning the religious dogma that was pounded into my head by the priests and nuns. Biking has been an opportunity to go inside and contemplate life's lessons; it is a form of meditation as I pedal along nature trails through parks and quiet recreation areas. It enables me to connect with my spiritual self in ways that church and religion failed to get my attention. Many of the thoughts that end up in my books bubble to the surface during long bike rides.

*Character Building* is intended to be an extension of the lessons explored in *The Bike Writer*, with beliefs, attitudes, and philosophies developed from my experiences. I am finding that the more I write, the more I learn about myself and the people in my life. Writing helps me to become aware of the larger context that surrounds our brief time on earth.

This book uses the alphabet as an organized structure for discussing some of the potential building blocks for developing character and experiencing a fuller, happier, richer life.

## Evolving

I like to think of life as being in constant motion. Earth is moving at a speed close to one thousand miles per hour as it rotates on its axis. Sitting still is not an option on a constantly moving planet.

In our daily lives, I believe we are always evolving (i.e., progressing, advancing, learning, growing), devolving (i.e., moving backward to a lower level of functioning), or revolving (i.e., spinning around in circles and not really getting anywhere). The purpose of this book is to look at potential building blocks that can inspire us to evolve in the direction of our full potential and to release those negative blocks that may cause us to devolve or revolve.

I enjoy competitive games, such as golf, tennis, baseball, basketball, football, soccer, hockey, track, swimming, gymnastics, and so on. They hook my ego in a relatively harmless, playful way. I do not always enjoy competitions that involve real life, such as wars, turf battles, personal feuds, nasty elections, legal skirmishes, or political power struggles. These competitions and conflicts involve the ego in potentially harmful ways. This is the reason I spent much of my legal career as a mediator and problem solver. Fighting has never been my first option.

I believe we are not here to be in competition with one another. There will always be someone who is richer, stronger, smarter, funnier, more popular, better-looking, more athletic, or more successful. Competition with others will never bring us more than temporary fulfillment. Rather, I believe we are here to be in competition with ourselves, focusing on being the smartest, strongest, kindest, most loving, happiest, healthiest, sanest, most helpful persons we can be, given the talents and resources at our disposal.

Golf is my second-favorite sport after biking. Like biking, golf is primarily an inner competition, and the challenges, frustrations, and ethical issues involved in golf provide an opportunity to build character.

## Labels

Since 2001 Jan and I have lived in Southwest Florida, in the heart of conservatism. I am sometimes asked about my political leanings. What is my label? Am I a conservative or a liberal? Am I Republican or Democrat? Am I Christian?

I do not think of myself in terms of labels. I prefer to think of myself as a free and independent thinker, open to life's experiences. I meet far too many Americans who have prematurely donated their brains to a religious leader, Fox News, talk radio personalities, CNN, or MSNBC. It is clear that they are no longer able to think for themselves, choosing to see life through someone else's eyes. I do not intend to donate my brain to any political, media, or religious bloc as long as I am still alive and able to think for myself. I think that is what our Creator intended when each of us was given a brain.

Each of the twenty-six chapters of the book asks questions of the reader, hopefully to stimulate thought and introspection involving our lives, our opinions and beliefs, and the choices we make or fail to make as we pass through this human experience called life. My goal is to explore a higher, more peaceful and fulfilling way to live (i.e., a life with depth and strength of character).

Many years ago, when I attended the Unity Church in Fort Wayne, Indiana, my favorite part of each service was the song "Let There Be Peace on Earth," written in 1955 by Jill Jackson Miller and Sy Miller. The song includes this line: "Let there be peace on earth, and let it begin with me." That line resonates with me. The word *peace* could be interchanged with *character*, and the impact would be the same. The point is that changing the world begins with changing ourselves. This is intended to be a journey of self-discovery.

# Chapter A

> What if I have the power
> To choose today's attitude?
> Would I really choose to be sour,
> In a nasty, unhappy mood?
> JB

Deposits into the character account:

## ATTITUDE

While practicing law in the nineties, I helped to found, and then served on the board of, the Network for Attitudinal Healing International, which was headquartered in Austin, Texas. NAHI connected Centers for Attitudinal Healing around the world, providing conferences, training, and support for staffs overwhelmed with people dealing with catastrophic issues. From this experience I learned the importance of attitude for my own physical, mental, emotional, and spiritual well-being. I consider attitude to be the underlying foundation for developing the building blocks of character.

My mentor, psychiatrist Dr. Jerry Jampolsky, formed the first Center for Attitudinal Healing in Tiburon, California.

Jerry's best-selling book *Love Is Letting Go of Fear* created public awareness of the center's work with children and adults diagnosed with life-threatening illnesses. His belief is that our mental attitude can actually affect physical health and dangerous medical conditions. Angry, fearful thoughts and feelings often lead to sickness and disease. Choosing to be peaceful and positive instead has the potential to heal physical ailments.

*Love Is Letting Go of Fear* was also an important resource for helping me through the emotional aspects of ending a twenty-year marriage. The end of my marriage felt like a life-threatening condition.

Attitude is generally defined as a way of thinking or feeling that affects our behavior toward ourselves, people, objects, situations, or ideas. An attitude can be positive or negative. We learn attitudes from the people around us and from our life experiences. However, we retain the freedom to choose our own attitude. Blaming other people or situations for a negative attitude is simply counterproductive to leading a happy life. Developing a consistently positive attitude can be an important building block for developing character. Other people may try to influence how we think and feel, but only we can decide the nature of our attitude.

A positive attitude can be a key to a better life. We can observe the attitudes of family members, coworkers, friends, and strangers who share our experience. It is easy to see the impact of a positive (or a negative) attitude on the lives of other people. The hard part is applying this lesson to our own internal mind-set. That, in a nutshell, is our challenge: to make good choices for ourselves. At the end of each chapter I have provided some provoking questions that may be helpful in meeting this challenge.

## Authority

There are other important A building blocks that are connected to character. For example, *authority* is generally defined as the right or ability to control thoughts, actions, and behavior—our own and sometimes those of other people. The word derives from *author*, and critical questions any adult ought to be asking themselves include the following: Who is the author of my life? Who writes the script that describes my life experience? If I am not the author of my own life, then to whom have I delegated the job? And why would I relinquish this important role to someone else?

I don't accept the concept that "God" is pulling our strings and we are merely along for the ride. We may be partners with our Higher Power in life's process, and divine guidance may be helpful in our decision-making. However, I believe that being the author of my own life is not only my right but also my God-given responsibility. A Higher Power may be available for help, but we ultimately choose our own way in life.

Being an authority is a state of mind. It is an individual choice that some of us make. No one designates us as the authority on any particular subject. We designate ourselves—or not. When I practiced law in Fort Wayne, Indiana, I found myself doing a lot of estate planning for clients. I decided to focus on educating myself on all aspects of this area of the law, and eventually I acknowledged to myself that I was a knowledgeable authority. Once I made that internal decision, I was invited to speak at estate-planning seminars, taught continuing legal education classes, and became recognized as an authority on the subject. My estate-planning practice expanded exponentially. It was my internal decision to be an authority that made it happen.

No one asked Jerry Jampolsky to be the founder of Attitudinal Healing. He became aware of the need for an arena that was supportive of healing attitudes among patients with life-threatening conditions. He didn't wait for someone else to do something about it. He accepted the responsibility and led the way forward. He became recognized as a leading authority because he did the work that was needed.

I have known other people who held all the credentials to be considered an authority but lacked the confidence or ambition to lead. Some of these folks like to complain about the people in charge, never recognizing their own potential role in the process.

## Authenticity

Authenticity is another key ingredient for character. We all know someone who feels phony or fake. This is the person who tries to impress you with their knowledge or name drops important people they may or may not know. (I once joked that if I mentioned Jesus Christ to one of my golf buddies, Ted's response would be that he used to fish with Jesus. He apparently knew everyone ever worth knowing.) Phony behavior is a sign of insecurity.

Being authentic is the opposite of phony. It means being genuine, honest, sincere, and real, thereby instilling confidence and trust. This inevitably leads to greater self-esteem, confidence, and a higher level of functioning. We have a sense of knowing when we are in the presence of an authentic person. Authenticity is a building block of character.

Interestingly, as we learn to live an authentic life, we attract like-minded authentic people into our lives. The people closest to us are our mirrors. If we look around and see inauthentic people, it may be time to work on improving our own authentic self.

## Awareness

Being aware of our state of consciousness is a necessity in order to recognize the way our own thoughts, ideas, beliefs, and conduct are affecting ourselves and the world around us. A state of awareness is not automatic and is sometimes elusive for people who tend to go through life in a fog. For some of us, being an aware person may require professional tutelage, effort, and practice.

About thirty-five years ago I was in counseling, trying to save a failing marriage. My counselor, Marie, suggested that I keep a journal of my feelings. After some futile attempts, it became clear that I was not really aware of my feelings. I was stuck in my head and having trouble getting to my heart. Our solution was for me to write down a list of potential feelings and carry the list with me, no matter what I was doing. My assignment was to be aware of when I was engaged in a feeling that was on my written list. That eventually worked for me, helping me to tune in to my feelings.

## Aging

People age differently and at different paces. Chronologically, of course, we all age at the same rate, getting one year older about every 365 days. Aging is not a positive or negative concept. It is a fact of life, and each one of us chooses what the experience is for us. Our attitude determines if we are carried kicking and screaming into old age, or if it is a mellow, rewarding experience that expands our character.

Some of the most interesting and enjoyable characters I have known were elderly clients in my law practice. A significant portion of my practice involved elder law issues, and elderly clients seemed to trust me.

A retired high school principal became a client. Pete was affectionately known as "Papa Bear" at the school, whose mascot was a bruin. He was famous for making announcements on the school's intercom system, identifying himself as Papa Bear. Pete was a highly respected educator, who was also able to connect with the students in his school. He loved to walk the halls and talk with the students. He was one of those lovable characters that everyone wanted to be around. His joy was contagious.

I had the privilege of doing some estate planning with Pete and his wife, after his retirement. Initially I quoted a legal fee of $800 for the work they needed. As I got to know them and share in their humor, we began to play little pranks on each other. They never left my office without several good belly laughs among the three of us. When the work was completed and signed, I presented them with a fake legal bill that included not only $800 in legal fees but also notary and witness fees, room charges, supply charges for paper clips and staples, and the like. The total fake bill was many times my initial quote of $800, but I carefully pointed out that legal fees were exactly what I told them they would be. They were still laughing when they got home and showed their neighbors and friends my bill. Thanks to Pete, I ended up representing much of the neighborhood. Pete was a character who had character, and he spread his joy for life to others. He aged like a fine wine.

The choices we make often impact the pace and quality of our aging process. People who live active, healthy lifestyles, maintaining a light and positive attitude, tend to age more gracefully than couch potatoes, alcohol or drug abusers, or highly stressed individuals. It seems to me that people who have character, like Pete, tend to age well.

## Assertiveness

Being assertive does not come natural to everyone. Some of us (me included) had assertiveness "beaten out of us" as children, as we were taught to be meek and obedient. In Ferdinand, children were to be seen and not heard. Assertive means that we confidently, directly, and clearly communicate our feelings, needs, and opinions. It can be the key to successful marriages, parenting, friendships, or business ventures. Assertion does not usually require being aggressive.

Withdrawals from the character account:

There are also some *A* blocks connected to attitude that can cause character flaws, resulting in withdrawals from the character account.

Abusing others or allowing ourselves to be abused can deplete our account. Abuse is broadly defined as hurting ourselves or someone else, mentally, emotionally, physically, or sexually. Being an abusive person, misusing power to cause harm, is a sure way to becoming a miserable, unhappy person who lacks character.

Attack is an aggressive or violent action intended to cause harm or gain an advantage. In the context of war or athletic contests, attack can be an effective strategy. In real life, there are common misperceptions that when we attack another person, we are exhibiting strength, and when we are defenseless, we are weak. In my opinion, the reverse is true. Only weak people bully or attack other people. Only insecure people belittle other people or call them derogatory names. People attack because they are afraid. It is a call for help. A strong person of character has no need to become offensive.

Character assassination of another person might temporarily boost our own ego; it is putting someone else down so we can feel superior. Persons with character do not feel the need to belittle, make fun of, or attach nasty labels to another person. Such behavior does not define the person being abased; it defines the assassin as a person lacking in character.

Anxiety is one of the more visible forms of fear. It is a nervous, apprehensive, uncomfortable, uneasy worry about something that might happen in the future. Being anxious can be a normal and justified response to an upcoming challenge, but an overreaction can destroy confidence and inner peace. Learning to release fearful anxiety can lead to inner strength and peace of mind, important launching pads for acquiring character.

When we are filled with anger, we are constantly feeling annoyed or even hostile. Anger often comes out at inappropriate times and in awkward ways. Angry people are rarely happy. Anger is an emotion rooted in fear, and it can destroy physical, mental, and emotional health. When an orange is squeezed, orange juice is the result. When an angry person is squeezed, rage is the result.

Being aloof can cause a lack of intimacy in relationships. An aloof partner can be seen as withdrawn and distant, uninvolved and uninterested in other people. There may be a connection between aloofness and shyness. Being aloof does not build character.

Everyone knows someone who is so self-absorbed or socially inept that they turn every conversation or comment into something about them. They seem to lack the interest or curiosity in other people involved in the situation. Instead, these people turn inward and personalize the discussion. Often, the "all about me" character lacks character.

**Questions to consider:**

Who do I think of as the author, director, and producer of my life?

How would I describe my attitude toward myself? Do I like who I am? If not, what would I change?

Who are the people in my life that demonstrate depth of character?

What can I learn from these persons of character?

Do I consider myself to be an angry person? If so, what am I angry about?

## Chapter B

> What if being my best
> Is really a personal test?
> Do I consider it essential
> To live up to my own potential?
> JB

Deposits into the character account:

## Being

In the busy, modern world we live in, it is sometimes tempting to measure the quality of our lives by what we do. We have become a society of human doings. We identify ourselves based on what we do for a living, the roles we play within our families, how well we perform in sports or hobbies, which organizations we support, how much money we make, and even how many items on our to-do list get done each day.

Beyond doing, our inner essence is being. It is our nature, our spirit, our state of consciousness, our character. It is the essence of our existence on earth—who we really are rather than what we do. It seems to me that humans have been trained to focus more easily on what we do than who we are. What we do may offer an external reflection of who we are, but it is not the genuine article.

If we begin to view ourselves and everyone else as human beings rather than human doings, how might it affect who we are? Would we be more forgiving of ourselves and others? Would we learn to tune in to our highest selves, our spiritual natures? Would we be kinder, gentler, and less judgmental? I think it would provide an entirely different picture of the world we live in.

## Biking

For me, all roads lead to biking. For seventy years biking has been a balancing influence in my life. For the past seventeen years, following heart bypass surgery, it has been my physical rehab. It has also been my private time for meditation. I bike almost every day, traveling in excess of six thousand miles per year. It is what I do, and it is also who I am. Long bike rides help to develop my character.

When I hop on my bike, my mind seems to split into two distinct parts. One part of my brain is aware of my physical surroundings, traffic, weather conditions, and the like. A deeper part of my consciousness is freed up to think about life and what matters most to me. Many of the ideas I write about float to the surface of my mind while I am biking. It is the reason I have dubbed these books *The Bike Writer Trilogy*.

Biking is one of my personal character-building blocks. For someone else it might be golf, jogging, tennis, hiking, teaching, bridge, cooking, gardening, religion, politics, carpentry, reading, family, friends, volunteer work, or hobbies. The key point is to find an effective vehicle that provides an entrance into who we are deep inside.

## Blessedness

For the last year or so, as I have biked south on Vanderbilt Drive on my way to a Naples destination, I have met a biker going in the opposite direction. This guy always shouts out, "Have a blessed day!" The first few times it happened, I chalked him up as a religious nut. However, the more often it happened, the more I realized that I kind of liked the message. It was his way of sharing his inner joy, and I felt blessed by him.

Blessedness is a state of well-being and contentment. It is a feeling of being connected to our divine source. I consider it to be an important building block. Maybe someday I will follow this biker's lead and shout his message to other bikers. Or maybe I won't; it doesn't really feel like my style. I will probably just wave and be friendly, stopping if someone needs help.

When we focus on the many blessings in our lives rather than the perceived lacks, the quality of life takes a huge leap upward. Feeling blessed is a state of mind that has little or nothing to do with what we have or what we do. It is a personal choice.

## Boldness

Being bold is a difficult challenge for many of us who have been bombarded with fears most of our lives. The courage to act boldly with a willingness to make mistakes, look foolish, and take risks is an important part of becoming our potential. Without people willing to explore adventures or dangers, our civilization would be a boring place in which to live.

Hans considered himself and his family trapped in East Berlin. It was not the kind of life he envisioned living. The only escape was over the Berlin Wall, which was heavily guarded by armed soldiers. His yearning for freedom and a better life awakened his inner boldness. After careful study and planning, they made their escape over the wall and immigrated to America. Their new lives in America were all they dreamed they would be.

## Bipartisanship

America is witnessing the demise of bipartisanship in the political sphere, whether in Washington, DC, state capitals, or county seats. The result is bickering, abuse of power, and a general inability to govern. When politicians refuse to cooperate with each other in order to find common ground, the people suffer the consequences.

There was a time in American politics when statesmen worked hard to reach commonsense agreements for the benefit of American citizens and the world. Perhaps such an era will come again in the not-too-distant future. We can only hope that our elected officials will regain a sense of character and a commitment to do the right thing in government.

Withdrawals from the character account:

I am aware of some *B* blocks that can have a detrimental impact on our character.

Bullying is high on the list of negative traits. Bullying is cruel, insulting, or threatening behavior toward another person. It is a form of aggressive behavior exercised by someone who perceives himself or herself to be in a position of power, able to control or harm someone who is weak and vulnerable.

Unfortunately, bullying is an all too common in grade school and high school. Most bullies grow out of it and learn to behave differently as they become adults; however, a few of them carry on their cruel behavior in business, politics, or family life. Bullies tend to be fearful, insecure people who try to come across as strong by threatening others. Bullies do not lead happy lives, and neither do their victims. Bullies lack character.

Similar to bullying, bigotry involves hatred and intolerance of ideas, races, religions, political beliefs, life styles, or opinions that are different from one's own. In my experience, bigots tend to be ignorant people who are fearful of anyone they perceive as different. The bigots I have known in my life have been miserable, unhappy, and sadly lacking in character.

Blaming others for our problems is also a sure step backward in our level of functioning. Being a victim of the world and failing to accept responsibility for our situation is definitely not a building block to developing character. Life is not always fair. Life is, however, always a personal test. A willingness to take responsibility for our lives is the only correct answer to the test.

**Questions to consider:**

Is my daily focus on my to-do list, or am I aware of the essence of my being?

Am I tuned into my true nature here and now?

What are the vehicles that I use to move in a positive direction in my life?

How willing am I to take a risk in order to grow?

Am I open to other points of view?

# Chapter C

*What if success is defined*
*By the thought process in my mind?*
*Would I choose thoughts of fear*
*Or replace them with the confident kind?*
JB

Deposits into the character account:

## Confidence

When I began writing my first book, *The Bike Writer*, I must admit that I had some doubts about my ability to complete the project. There were a lot of questions running through my mind on a daily basis: What could I possibly have to share that someone else would want to read? How do I organize my thoughts to make logical sense? Can I come up with enough material to make the project worthwhile? What if someone reads the book and doesn't like my message? How will I react? Will I feel hurt or defensive? How do I ever get the dumb thing published? Am I going to look stupid for the effort? Is it a waste of my time?

Fortunately I live in a kind, supportive environment. I am blessed with a wife, family, and friends who encouraged me to take the plunge. They believed in my ability to write the book, and their encouragement added to my confidence to move forward.

In truth, writing a book is more about the internal process of the author than it is about the reaction of readers. It was a learning process each step of the way, and each step gave me additional confidence that the project was worthwhile. Overcoming blocks, releasing fears, and changing attitudes were daily challenges. The editing process with my publisher was an exercise in patience and not getting defensive.

In retrospect, writing *The Bike Writer* was one of the most positive experiences of my life. It helped me to see myself from a different perspective. It gave me confidence far beyond my ability to write books. It added to my depth of character.

Playing golf is a close second to my love of biking. Unlike biking, which I love unconditionally, I have a love/hate relationship with golf, depending on how well I am playing on any particular day. One of my favorite golf books is *Golf Is Not a Game of Perfect* by Dr. Bob Rotella. One of Dr. Rotella's concepts is that people become what they think about themselves. I can think of myself as an excellent golfer or a born loser. If I am confident over a golf shot, I will probably hit a good shot. If I lack confidence, I am in trouble. Golf is a miniature version of life.

## Commitment

When I am confident, I am more willing to commit myself to something or someone. Commitment involves dedication, faithfulness, and responsibility. It means making conscious choices and carrying through on promises. It is the opposite of wishy-washy or being a flip-flopper.

Many important aspects of life require a willingness to commit. It is an essential part of a successful marriage or relationship, effective parenting, building a career, or writing a book. Commitment is also a crucial ingredient in building character. People who are unable to commit tend to drift through life without a mission, purpose, goals, or moral compass.

Randy was a brilliant student majoring in chemistry, and he lived down the hall from me in Upper Linden Hall at Indiana University. He came from an extremely poor family and was working his way through college with scholarships and earnings from part-time jobs. After his sophomore year of college, he earned a summer internship with a chemical company located in Northern Indiana on the shores of Lake Michigan. One day, on an outing with friends, Randy dove into a shallow part of Lake Michigan. He broke his neck and was partially paralyzed as a result of his injuries. I had the opportunity to visit Randy at his parents' home a few months after his accident, and I thought his life was over. He was bedridden and could not walk or move around. Randy, however, had other ideas.

Randy spent two years at home, rehabbing to ease his paralysis and regain limited movement. He eventually changed his major from chemistry to prelaw. He graduated from law school and went on to a successful career as an attorney. He was totally committed to developing his potential despite the formidable obstacles placed in his way. Randy had depth of character.

## Contentment

To be content is to be happy and satisfied. It involves peace of mind, which has more to do with our attitude and character than it does with the external conditions of our lives.

Contentment does not mean a lack of ambition or drive. It does not meaning being passive.

It is possible to be financially successful beyond our wildest dreams but lack a feeling of contentment. For the ego, there is never enough. It is equally possible to have very little but to be grateful and content with what we have.

When we are content, we are not envious of others or whining about how unfair life is. We appreciate the here and now of life, knowing it is a divine present. Contentment and the ego tend to be mutually exclusive.

## Civility

Civility and respect go hand in hand. Civility involves genuine behavior that is polite, courteous, and respectful. It means being nice and friendly to everyone, friend or foe. Civility has been sadly lacking in the realm of American partisan politics, and this uncivil style of leadership appears to be trickling down into other aspects of life in America.

Washington, DC, has become the epicenter of incivility, and that needs to change for America to move forward as a civilization. We are in desperate need of political leaders with character, who are committed to doing the right thing. Partisan politics is tearing this nation apart, and it is long past due to begin the healing process.

My niece, Sue, recently emceed a discussion at Butler University in Indianapolis that featured former senator Richard Lugar and former congressman Lee Hamilton. The topic was the need for civility in government. These two gentlemen were products of a different era in Washington, when respect and civility trumped partisan bickering.

Civility (or incivility) is contagious. When we treat people with respect, they reciprocate. When people are nice to us, we return the favor. It is a vicious cycle. If our country's leaders are unwilling to demonstrate civility, then perhaps it is time for a grassroots movement of ordinary citizens to show them the way.

### Courage

The great boxer Muhammad Ali once said, "He who is not courageous enough to take risks will accomplish nothing in life." Courage is the strength to persist in the face of a difficult challenge. It is the ability to overcome fears in order to accomplish our goals. Ali, himself, practiced what he preached.

It takes character and courage to stand up and speak out for an unpopular political position that nevertheless represents a "true north" principle. The easy thing is to keep quiet and not make waves so that no one will challenge our position. Without courage the United States would not have entered into European wars in the twentieth century that saved Western civilization as we know it. If activists had not had the courage to march, the Civil Rights Act would never have become the law of the land and the Vietnam War might still be going on. Courage is an American tradition and a cherished value.

### Calmness

Calmness of mind is an underrated building block for character. In a world that values hyperactive, busy, stress-filled lives, it can feel like an oasis to be in the company of a calm, peaceful person. Releasing thoughts of anger, fear, worry, and guilt can make room for inner calmness. Calmness eliminates the urge to sigh, whine, complain, or blame. It allows room for character to expand.

Alberto is a medical doctor in Buenos Aires, Argentina, and he and I served together on the board of the Network for

Attitudinal Healing International more than twenty years ago. I have never forgotten what it felt like to be around Alberto. He was a calming presence in the midst of stress and conflict. Everyone on the board admired and respected his leadership and his peaceful consciousness. Alberto is an influential leader because he exudes an inner peace.

## Caring

Having concern for our fellow human beings is a valuable attribute that demonstrates strength of character. It is relatively easy to care for a relative or friend with whom we have a personal connection. Blessed are those among us who look after the less fortunate in our lives.

Becoming a nurse was a natural career path for Ann to follow. Her life was always dedicated to caring for others. After many years as a hospital nurse, Ann eventually turned to hospice nursing. She wanted to help patients make their transition a meaningful part of life, and she helped the patients' families and loved ones to appreciate the experience. Ironically, Ann became a hospice patient as a result of a long battle with breast cancer, and she continued to make her dying process a positive learning experience for her husband and daughters.

## Conservative

Long before *conservative* was a political label, conserving was a noncontroversial personality trait. It meant saving, being frugal, and not wasting resources. Being ecologically conservative means being responsible for our lifestyle, protecting natural resources, recycling, and making do with less.

Politically, Dan and Andrea are far from conservative. However, they live their minimalist lifestyle as careful stewards of earth's precious resources. Water and electricity are used only as absolutely needed, and they don't need a trash bin, as every item is recycled. They are role models for being truly conservative.

## Choice

We make choices every instant of every day. Every thought, feeling, or action represents a choice that we consciously or subconsciously make. The choices we make determine the quality of our lives on an accumulative basis. The more good choices we make, the better life becomes. Bad choices usually result in misery, sadness, fear, loneliness, and the like.

The trick is to be as aware as we can possibly be of the choices we are making on an ongoing basis. As Robert Frost so eloquently put it in "The Road Not Taken": "Two roads diverged in a woods, and I—I took the one less traveled by, and that has made all the difference."

Withdrawals from the character account:

Not all *C* words are positive building blocks for a better life. For example, cheating at anything is an excellent way to diminish our own character and life experience. Whether we cheat in relationships, business, financial matters, or golf, the consequence is similar: our self-esteem takes a hit, and our reputation suffers. Cheating inevitably returns full circle to bite the cheater in the butt.

Corruption is a form of cheating that seems to permeate politics, whether at the local, state, or national level. Our prisons are populated by corrupt politicians who have managed to ruin their own lives and the lives of their family and friends in order to profit illegally from their official position.

Even the corrupt politicians who have avoided prosecution are suffering from guilt, fear, and low self-esteem.

Vanity, narcissism, egotism, and conceit are all too evident among our nation's leaders. These are traits that most people do not admire. Normal people have an innate sense of distaste for this type of personality and do their best to avoid such people. There is no room for character in a mind that is excessively proud of one's self. Self-confidence builds character; self-aggrandizement destroys character.

**Questions to consider:**

How confident am I in my ability to accomplish a goal?

What can I do to increase my level of confidence?

Am I treating my family members, friends, coworkers, and strangers with kindness and respect?

Am I willing to stand up and be counted for what I believe?

Who and what are the things that I care about the most?

## Chapter D

*What if being defenseless*
*Is really a wise move to make?*
*No need to build up defenses,*
*No matter the issue at stake!*
JB

Deposits into the character account:

## Defenselessness

Practicing law too often involves a vicious cycle of attacking and defending. It is often adversarial in nature, with attorneys playing the role of hired guns. In the early years of my practice I hated the fighting and blaming, but I felt trapped. After a few unpleasant years of practice, I decided to refocus my legal career on problem solving instead of fighting. That decision probably saved my life.

When a corporate client let me know that a former employee had opened a competing business and was using promotional materials that were nearly identical to his, I wrote a letter to the former employee, asking her to change her logo and designs so that customers would not be confused or misled as to which company they were dealing with. A few days later I received a phone call from her attorney, during which he yelled and screamed at me for a good thirty minutes, while (I suspect) his client sat across the desk from him. I listened politely, occasionally asking questions to keep him venting. When he finally took a breath, I thanked him for expressing his feelings and suggested that we all meet in his office to discuss possible solutions. He immediately calmed down.

When we met at his office, all his venom had been spent. I think he was embarrassed by his behavior on the phone. He and his client graciously agreed to make the changes as we requested, and the matter was resolved. It was a perfect example of being defenseless—no expensive lawsuits and no hard feelings.

## Determination

It takes character to persist, to continue to try to achieve something that may be difficult. Determination involves clarity and a sense of purpose. We all know people who take on a task and then abandon the project when hardships arise. We also know folks who steadfastly follow their dreams, working diligently to complete their education, develop their careers, build their businesses, raise their families, finish the project, or recover from serious injuries, illnesses, or addictions. Very few people succeed in life without a strong sense of determination.

The polio epidemic was in full bloom in the early fifties, and my next-door neighbor contracted this dreaded disease. Herb had been a plumber, and he now spent many months paralyzed and confined to his bedroom. It seemed his life was over. Herb, however, never gave up. Eventually he recovered enough to be able to move around with the help of crutches and metal braces on both legs. His car was refitted so that the accelerator and brake could be operated with his hands.

Herb was determined to live his life, and he restarted his plumbing business with a small plumbing and heating supply store on Main Street. He hired a plumber to do his legwork. Herb was able to provide for his wife and three children and enjoyed many years of independent living despite his plight. Herb had grit, determination, and character. He was loved and admired by everyone who knew him. He made a very big impression on me, and I will never forget his demonstration of character.

## Depth

To me, *depth* means wisdom, insight, intelligence, and complexity. We are drawn to people we sense have personal depth of character. They tend to be interesting, multitalented, logical and/or creative thinkers, and genuine. A deep sense of openness, caring, and curiosity emanates from their personality. They are usually good listeners, understanding the needs of others. They are good friends to have in our lives.

I had a tax professor in law school who exemplified depth of character. He was probably the smartest person I have ever known, but his intelligence was not his primary talent. Larry was not only one of the world's leading experts on taxation, but he cared deeply for his students. He would do anything in his power to help them to succeed. He got to know each student in his class as a person, and he often knew our spouses and children as well. No student showed up in his classroom unprepared for the lesson. We did not want to disappoint the teacher.

Larry maintained a relationship with his students long after they graduated. He referred many clients to me, and

I got him involved in tax issues that exceeded my level of expertise. Fifteen years after our last class together, Larry invited me and my son, Mike, to be his guests for the Indy 500 race. I was not a race fan, but we would not have missed the experience for the world. It was a chance to spend time with a great friend. Larry had (and still has) depth of character. He is making a positive difference in his world.

## Daring

A willingness to be adventurous and daring is an important ingredient of character. The persons of character that I have known have not been boring or stuck in ruts. They are willing to look at the world and their lives from different perspectives, exploring new options and ways of doing things. They are not afraid of failing, knowing that failures can be the catalyst for personal growth and learning.

Being daring requires a willingness to change, think differently, and be open to possibilities. Being daring is not the same as being a daredevil who takes risk for the excitement of the challenge, like walking a tightrope between skyscrapers. To me, daring involves weighing the costs and the benefits, doing the necessary preparations, and moving forward in worthwhile ventures.

America as we know it was founded by Europeans who dared to cross the dangerous Atlantic Ocean to begin new lives in a wilderness. The West was developed by pioneers daring to cross the country on horseback or in covered wagons. It takes a spirit of daring to start a family, build a business, move away from home, or be an entrepreneur. These activities can be character building.

## Doing the Right Thing

Doing the right thing means different things to different people. Doing the right thing may mean telling the truth about knowing there may be adverse consequences, admitting a mistake and apologizing for it, or making an extra effort to help someone in need.

When I was about twelve years old, the parents of my best friend opened a small grocery store to compete with the only established grocery store in town. It was an uphill battle from the outset, and a few years later they had exhausted their savings and were forced to liquidate the store. They paid as many creditors as they could and discharged the balance of their debt in bankruptcy.

However, that was not the end of their story. Both parents took factory jobs and worked as much overtime as they could, living frugally and saving their money. Within five years they were able to repay all the debts that had been legally discharged in bankruptcy. They felt that was the right thing to do.

And they weren't finished yet. They continued to work long hours to help their two children go to college. When they finally retired, they did not have a big retirement nest egg, but they had the respect of everyone in the community—and perhaps more importantly, they had self-respect. They demonstrated a depth and strength of character that set a high standard for their children to follow. The contrast with billionaire business people who routinely use the bankruptcy laws to avoid paying their creditors is stunning.

Withdrawals from the character account:

Being defensive can be an obstacle to developing character. When we are defensive, we are not open to change or growth. Defensiveness is an emotion that emanates from fear, which is perhaps the greatest challenge that any of us face in life. If we are not careful and aware, it can become a habitual reaction.

Deception is the hiding of the truth. It is intended to mislead or trick someone. Deception can be an effective tool in football, when the quarterback fakes a pass and then hands the ball to a running back. In real life, being deceitful is generally not a positive character trait. Defrauding someone under false pretenses can result in a prison sentence. Deception is the opposite of honesty and erodes character.

When a sleazy politician manipulates facts or circumstances to play on peoples' emotions or prejudices, that politician is practicing demagoguery. He or she appeals to the worst nature of people, exploiting ignorance and prejudice. Being a demagogue is inconsistent with character building, and it doesn't help the people being manipulated either.

Being duplicitous is also not helpful in building character. Duplicity involves deception, underhandedness, fraud, trickery, and so forth. A con artist or a dishonest sales person may be guilty of duplicity. Dishonesty may build bank accounts, but it does not build character accounts.

**Questions to consider:**

Do I react defensively when someone makes accusations or blames me for a problem?

Do I have an open mind to other perspectives and possibilities?

How does doing the right thing make me feel?

How does failing to do the right thing make me feel?

# CHAPTER E

*What if our nose is the guide*
*To living with nothing to hide?*
*Does the situation addressed*
*Pass the smell test?*
JB

Deposits into the character account:

## ETHICAL BEHAVIOR

Many professional associations have codes of ethics that govern acceptable behavior by members of the profession. Contrary to popular belief, violation of ethical rules can get an attorney disbarred. Medical doctors can lose the right to practice medicine as a result of unethical conduct. There is an unwritten code of ethics that guides the acceptable conduct of all members of society in any civilization. Most of us recognize unethical behavior when we see it.

My wife, Jan, has a commonsense approach to the question of ethics: Does the situation or course of conduct pass the smell test? If a proverbial foul odor emanates from the activity, stay as far away as possible, unless your goal is to develop a stinky character. Do not participate in anything that smells foul, no matter how attractive the temptation might appear. It's a slippery slope to nowhere good.

## Enlightenment

The Dark Ages was an era in European history that involved intellectual suppression and barbarity. It began about the fifth century and was a time of religious persecution, violence, torture, poverty, suffering, and fear. The Catholic Church was the most powerful institution in Europe during the Dark Ages. It was a time of very few scientific advancements, scholarly writings, or creative artwork. The Dark Ages was the flip side of enlightenment.

Not surprisingly, the darkness was followed by the Renaissance and the Age of Discovery. The ensuing centuries brought scientific discoveries, agricultural advancements, important writings, and creativity in art and architecture. Great cathedrals and monasteries were built all over Europe. The printing press was invented, leading to a proliferation of books and writings.

Science and logic became alternatives to religious control and narrow ways of thinking. The Age of Enlightenment gave rise to philosophers such as Descartes and Newton and emphasized the importance of science and human reasoning. Enlightenment is an awakening, an openness to new thoughts and ideas—key ingredients for depth of character.

## Empathy

Empathy is the ability to identify with and understand the feelings and emotional state of someone else. It means getting beyond our own narcissistic mind-set. Empathy requires an ability to share what it would be like to be in the other person's shoes. Empathy is an important quality for a spouse, family member, or friend to have. Without empathy, we don't feel connected as human beings.

I was barely sixteen years old when my dad died of colon cancer. He died in our home after several months of his body wasting away. My sister Ann was a registered nurse and moved in with us to take care of Dad through his dying process.

There was a lot going on within our family as a result of Dad's death. As the youngest member of the family, I felt lost in the shuffle, with no one to talk to. I felt left out of the process, with lots of questions but no one available. All my older siblings were busily involved in their own lives, and I was the only one still living at home.

My brother Joe was a college student and he had a roommate named Phil. Phil hitchhiked almost one hundred miles to attend our dad's funeral. He understood the grief we were feeling and wanted to be there for us. After the funeral, Joe and I drove Phil back to his home so he would not have to hitchhike back. On that car trip, I was able to express my grief and fears, and Phil and Joe listened to me and gave me the feedback I needed. I felt what empathy was like, and I will never forget the importance of that car trip with my brother and his friend. It changed my life.

## Environment

Environment means more than my physical surroundings. It includes the conditions in which I live, the people who surround me, the attitudes and consciousness of the surrounding society, and the philosophies and behaviors of everyone who may have an impact on my life. An environment can be friendly or dangerous; it can be encouraging or suppressive; it can be nurturing or destructive.

We have choices when we are in an environment that is inconsistent with our values. We can feel trapped, adapt, attempt to change the environment, or remove ourselves from the undesirable situation. I have experienced all the above at various points in my life when I found myself in an environment that was less than healthy.

Some people are strong enough to thrive in a nasty environment. I am not one of them. It makes sense to me to choose to live in a different environment that includes people I admire and respect. More often than not, I have chosen the escape route from undesirable environments. Choosing to live in a friendly, nurturing environment can make all the difference when it comes to building character.

## Empowerment

In the world of business, the best managers are the ones who have the ability to empower their coworkers. Empowerment means helping someone to become stronger and more confident. It often requires sharing information, delegating responsibilities, mentoring, and allowing the freedom for initiative to flourish.

It takes a confident leader to empower others, a leader with strength of character. John was a college football coach with a successful track record. Miami of Ohio, Indiana University, and Northwestern University were all beneficiaries of his presence. When John retired, he and his wife bought a condo in Bonita Springs, Florida, and we played some golf together.

John once told me that the key to his successful coaching career was hiring good assistant coaches and empowering them to do their jobs. His goal was to teach them to be successful so that they could leave his program and become head coaches at other colleges. He became known as the "father of coaches" because so many of his assistant coaches moved on to head coach positions. As a result, John was able to attract new, talented assistant coaches. John had character.

Withdrawals from the character account:

An inflated ego is an obstacle to character. The ego is that part of the mind that governs our self-esteem and sense of self-worth. It is our self-image—the opinion we have about ourselves. When that self-image gets distorted into an inflated sense of self-importance, we say that the person is egotistical or even narcissistic. Narcissists have a great need for attention and admiration. They can never get enough of either.

Emoting endlessly by complaining, whining, sighing, or expressing the unfairness of life does not build a character account. Accepting life's circumstances is a much better way to live.

The human mind is capable of rationalizing almost anything. We can always find some excuse for conduct that is less than acceptable. Making excuses for poor choices causes a steady erosion of a character account.

## Questions to consider:

How well do I connect with the feelings of other people?

Do I truly respect the people in my life?

Do I expect ethical behavior by government, business, and religious leaders?

Am I willing to empower the people around me, or do I need all the credit?

## Chapter F

> What if my own peace of mind
> Depends on a willingness to let go,
> To dismiss actions deemed as unkind,
> To go high when someone goes low?
> JB

Deposits into the character account:

## FORGIVENESS

As a child indoctrinated in the Catholic system, I was taught that I was an unworthy, miserable sinner and only God, through His priest in the confessional box, could grant my forgiveness. Even then, I had to earn the forgiveness by confessing my "sins," followed by a penance of many prayers. That was my introduction to the concept of forgiveness.

As an adult I've learned that forgiveness is a much deeper topic than the confessional. It has to begin with forgiving ourselves. We cannot give something we do not possess. Until we are willing to forgive ourselves, it is doubly difficult to forgive someone else. The sixth Principle of Attitudinal Healing is as follows: We can learn to love ourselves and others by forgiving rather than judging.

True forgiveness is different from a pardon from a superior person to an inferior person. It is not preceded with condemnation. True forgiveness brings peace to both the forgiver and the forgiven.

True forgiveness builds character. Many years ago I was mediating a difficult divorce. The couple had two small children and was trying hard to be civil to each other for the sake of the children. Unfortunately, the wife was having a hard time forgiving her husband for a situation that led up to their separation. As long as she held on to the resentment, it was an uneasy truce between the two of them. She was angry, and he felt guilty. The children could feel the tension between their parents.

The wife's marriage counselor asked her to consider forgiving her husband for her own benefit; it would be a way for her to release the anger and regain a sense of inner peace. After weeks of struggle and prayer, she was able to reach the point of true forgiveness. The tension was released and they were able to coparent their children at a high level. Forgiveness freed her to move on with her life and eventually into a rewarding new relationship. Forgiveness was a large deposit into her own personal character account.

## Faith

For me, faith is not about a blind adherence to any particular religious dogma. One faith or religious teaching is not necessarily superior to another faith or teaching. Rather, my faith is based on an inner knowing that everyone I meet on my life path is a spiritual being, and we are in each other's life for a reason. We travel on this human journey together. Each person is deserving of my respect and love, regardless of their religious background, color of skin, personality, occupation, place of origin, sexual orientation, or language. I have faith that there is more to life than the physical world I see with my eyes.

When we are narrow-minded and prejudiced, our character fails to get the nourishment it needs to flourish. Our faith suffers from arrested development. When we are open to diversity and different points of view, we are exposing our character to opportunities to grow and develop. Faith and character need all the fresh air they can get.

## Freedom

Freedom is the right to be ourselves. Freedom is not free and cannot be taken for granted. Over history, many brave people have suffered and died to protect our right to be free. It has been an expensive process, and it would be a shame to waste our freedom.

Religious freedom, the right to free speech, free press, and the right to bear arms are some of the precious freedoms treasured in America. More importantly, one of America's unheralded but basic freedoms is the right to choose our thoughts. We get to decide who and what we will be; how we will act; what we will say; what we decide to believe in; and whether or not we will exercise our freedom of religion. We can choose where we will live our lives and with whom we live. It may not always seem like it, but we choose our career paths and our friends and relationships. Human beings are driven by their free thoughts.

We are free to tell the truth or to lie; to give or to take; to be fearful or loving; to be helpful or hurtful; to be productive or lazy. We have the freedom to choose, and the choices we make on a daily basis determine the quality of our lives and the content of our character.

## Fairness

A sense of fairness is an ability to understand all sides of a situation and to behave in a manner that is appropriate for all concerned. Fairness is a freedom from bias, favoritism, partiality, prejudice, or injustice. Life is not always fair, but in America fairness is the ultimate goal.

We expect fairness in athletic competitions, with impartial referees or umpires. We also expect fairness in daily life, including the way we are treated by law enforcement officials, as consumers of business services and products, or for the work we do. Fairness is a part of the fabric of our American system, and when it is absent, it adversely affects all of us.

Current political life has determined that fairness is out of date. Too many politicians have set aside their consciences and have embarked on selfish, exploitive paths that have their constituencies shaking their collective heads in disbelief.

We know when we have treated someone unfairly, and it always results in a withdrawal from our character account. The unfair person is the real loser.

## Focus

People who have the ability to focus, to concentrate intensely, are more apt to attain their goals in life. Distractions abound in daily life, and it is not always easy to focus on a particular goal. Multitasking has become a way of life and a challenge to the ability to focus.

Businesses and politicians often establish focus groups to concentrate on one particular project or problem. Everyone in the group becomes focused on the same issue, and together they are more likely to come up with answers.

I enjoy watching professional golfers who seem to have an uncanny ability to block out every distraction, from an unruly crowd to changing weather conditions to aches and pains. I can see it in their eyes, as they focus entirely on the swing of the golf club. Jack Nicklaus was a master of focus. Tiger Woods could do it. Today I see it in the eyes of many young professionals, including Jason Day, Justin Johnson, and Jordan Spieth, the new generation of the best golfers in the world.

## Fun

Without the joy of having fun, life would be dull. Laughter and joy are key ingredients for building character. The more we enjoy life, the more likely we will be to actively participate in it and function at our highest level, no matter how serious the issue might be.

My family understood the importance of being light and funny. Life was not always easy, especially during the Great Depression, with a large family to house and feed. My parents were very serious about their responsibilities, but there was always lots of laughter, joking around, and pranks. I learned from the funniest people I know.

My sister Ann was twelve years older than me. We were both born on Groundhog Day, but twelve years apart. For all practical purposes, Ann was my mother for the first six years of my life. I was her constant companion, and she was my best friend. She had a contagious giggle, and I caught it. People could hear us coming from a block away.

Many years later, when Ann was a hospice nurse, our mother moved into Ann's home for the final two years of her life; Ann took great care of her. When my wife and I would visit them, there was always laughter and joy. Complaints were never part of the visit. They continued to joke around with each other until the very end. There was laughter even in death.

Over the years, when our family members get together, it is like a party, no matter the circumstance. Even funerals can include lightheartedness, laughter, and storytelling about the recently deceased. So far I have lost two parents and four siblings from my family of origin; just three of us are left. The pain of loss and the fun of gathering go hand in hand. They are not mutually exclusive.

## Friendliness

It never hurts to be friendly with another person. When biking, I make it a point to acknowledge fellow bikers, walkers, joggers, and motorists I meet along the way. I wave and talk to landscapers who are mowing, edging, and trimming the yards of the neighborhood. It takes no more time or effort to be friendly than it does to ignore the other people along the way. The smiles and acknowledgments I get in return make it well worth the effort. Being friendly, and being a good friend, tends to build character.

Withdrawals from the character account:

Fear is easily the greatest stumbling block to leading a full, rich life of character. Many psychologists agree that fear is the primary emotion behind other negative emotions. We may fear God, hell, death, rejection, being judged, looking stupid, or financial disasters. Personal fears can manifest as shyness, stress, worry, depression, anger, arrogance, bullying, defensiveness, greed, bigotry, or inaction. Overcoming fear can be a lifelong process for many of us. It is worth the effort.

Some people live their lives under false pretenses. They pretend they are someone they are not. Art became the manager of a golf club that had been acquired by his company.

The company had formed a limited liability company to assume the bank debt on the property, and Art, along with his cohorts, promised to revitalize and beautify the golf course. It was promised to be "better than Augusta."

Jan and I considered joining the club. Art told us that he and all his company executives were born-again Christians we could trust completely. That was a warning signal to us, and we passed on the membership. Real Christians don't talk the talk; they walk the walk.

Over the course of the next five years, our suspicions were confirmed, as Art and his company squeezed every ounce of cash out of the golf course, while failing to reinvest in the property. They behaved like a slum landlord. With the golf course in shambles, their company then walked away from the bank debt and left the members with nothing but empty promises. They were perfect examples of not being who they pretended to be.

Principle 7 of the Principles of Attitudinal Healing is: We can become love finders rather than faultfinders. Someone who habitually finds fault, grumbling and complaining their way through life, is not a fun person to be around. Such people lack character.

**Questions to consider:**

How willing am I to forgive myself?

How willing am I to forgive other people?

What does faith mean to me?

Do I have a highly developed sense of fairness?

What are my greatest fears?

Am I having fun yet?

# Chapter G

> What if our lives have been blessed
> By strangers and people we know,
> As we pass through our lives on a quest,
> Supporting cast safely in tow?
> JB

Deposits into the character account:

## GRATITUDE

In the course of our daily lives, we are not always fully aware of our many blessings. We take many things for granted and simply expect them to be there for us. Being aware and grateful is an important step toward building character. Expressing gratitude is a way of assuring blessings in the future.

Blessings flow into our lives in the form of friendships, support, material comforts, success-filled ventures, and meaningful, enjoyable experiences. Being grateful is an inner state of consciousness that recognizes the blessing and understands the significance of the situation. It is nearly impossible to feel grateful when we are focused on lack, fear, anger, envy, or comparing ourselves with others. No matter our situation, we can always feel grateful for something. It is the opposite of self-pity.

After a long and successful career in banking, while raising a remarkable family, Bob was diagnosed with a serious health challenge. At the age of eighty-five he had to go on dialysis to sustain his life. He has been on dialysis for the past four years, going through the procedure three times per week. It is obviously a difficult and unpleasant experience, but Bob chooses to focus on the wonderful nurses and technicians that are now an important part of his life, the relentless support of his wife and children, and the fact that medical technology allows him to continue to enjoy many aspects of life even as he approaches ninety years of age. He has made a conscious choice to be grateful rather than to complain. This is just another deposit into Bob's already overflowing character account.

## Generosity

Being generous is not all about money. It is a giving state of consciousness that involves sharing our talents, energy, material possessions, and money. Kahlil Gibran said, "And there are those who give and know not pain in their giving, nor do they seek joy, nor give mindfulness of virtue; they give as in yonder valley the myrtle breathes its fragrance into space, through the hands of such as these God speaks, and from behind their eyes He smiles upon the Earth."

Generosity is the opposite of greed. Ironically, the more we give, the more we receive. The most generous people in the world often end up being the wealthiest as well.

Otto was not a rich man by today's standards. He worked hard to raise seven children, most of the children having been born during the Great Depression. That didn't prevent him from helping families in his small town and surrounding area that were struggling financially. When he became aware of a problem, he met with the family to determine what they needed.

Otto meticulously avoided getting credit for his generosity, making his gifts as anonymously as possible in a small town. Even his family was unaware of some of his giving until the recipient families showed up at his funeral and told Otto's wife and children about his generous gifts to help them through difficult times. The family heard such testimonials as "We would have lost our house if Otto had not intervened" and "Our children would not have received any Christmas presents that year if it weren't for Otto." It was no coincidence that Otto was a man of impeccable character.

## Grace

I am unable to listen to the hymn "Amazing Grace" without tears forming in my eyes and a chill running up and down my spine. I feel that grace runs deeper than human activity. It involves a spiritual aspect, divine participation in the human activity. When I see grace in action, I sense a joint effort of the human and the spirit underlying the human.

Grace manifests itself in courtesy, poise, respect, elegance, and forgiveness. We love being in the presence of grace. It feels like a touch of the divine presence. Demonstrating grace, especially under pressure, can add to the level of a character account.

Being a graceful winner of a political or a sporting contest tells us a lot about the character of the winner. Being a graceful loser of that same contest tells us even more about the character of the losing party. Grace and a large ego are mutually exclusive.

## Genuineness

It would seem that being genuine would be a natural talent not that difficult to achieve. It means being ourselves, free from hypocrisy, manipulation, or dishonesty. Unfortunately, some religions and societies teach us that we are not good enough as we are and we need to present ourselves to others as someone else.

Pretending to be someone else can be an exhausting, stressful way to live. We all know people who try to be too cute or glib in order to hide their true selves. It is hard to get to know a person who is incapable of being genuine. There is no way to connect with a counterfeit personality.

Being genuine does not mean that we can't try to be a better person. Working on improvement is a legitimate human endeavor that is with us our entire lifetime; it is what this book is all about. But trying to hide who we are under layers of masks and subterfuge is not the answer to being real and genuine.

## Golfing

As a test of physical, mental, and emotional concentration, the ancient game of golf is unsurpassed. Playing golf can be fun, exciting, exhilarating, and satisfying. It can also be frustrating, excruciating, painful, humbling, difficult, scary, and depressing. In other words, the game of golf is an awful lot like life.

Golf can teach us confidence, mental toughness, inner peace, and how to stay in the present moment. The second a golfer moves from the process of the swing to thinking about a previous shot or future result is the very second that the game falls apart. It's all about focus on here and now.

Golfers are expected to keep their own score and call their own rules infractions, thereby choosing the level of their integrity and character. Played correctly, the game of golf is an excellent character builder.

Withdrawals from the character account:

Grandiosity is a mask for despair. It is the inflation of the ego, comparing ourselves as superior to other people. It is based on the fear that we are not good enough. Grandiosity does not build character. Grandiosity is much different from grandeur, which is the recognition that we are spiritual beings created by a Higher Power.

Guilt was an important aspect of Catholicism when I was a small child. We were taught that we were miserable sinners, guilty of our own sins as well as the Original Sin committed by Adam and Eve. It is a concept based on fear. Fortunately, as an adult I escaped from that form of religious message. Irrational guilt and shame can cause emotional paralysis. We cannot know that we are spiritual beings as long as guilt rules our lives.

Greed is another fear-based trait that fails to build character. It is a selfish desire for more, even at the expense of others. Greed is different from a prosperity consciousness, which is based on the idea that our thoughts create our experiences in life. Prosperity consciousness involves transforming thoughts of lack into thoughts of abundance. It is the difference between a slum landlord who ruthlessly squeezes poor tenants without taking care of the property and a landlord who takes pride in providing well-maintained housing for happy tenants.

**Questions to consider:**

Do I envy the success of my friends or relatives?

How is grace manifested in my life?

Do I carry feelings of guilt with me on my journey through life?

Who is the most generous person I know?

# Chapter H

What if a sense of humor
Is really a double-edged sword—
It can cut someone down like a tumor
Or lift someone up from the floor?
JB

Deposits into the character account:

# Humor

It is an old saying that laughter is good for the soul. It can also be good for character building. There are two distinct forms of humor: humor that is uplifting, amusing, and entertaining; and humor that is at someone's expense. The latter form of humor usually does not build character.

Dave is one of the funniest guys I know. He's never met a stranger, and he entertains people wherever he goes. Not too many years after WWII, Dave and a partner opened for business in an old Quonset. He built this business based on humor, creating and performing his own television ads. People never forgot his television ads or his entertaining sense of humor when they visited his store. Dave's humor was always on display, and the business flourished.

For many years Dave and I golfed and played tennis together several times a week. Every game was filled with laughs, never at anyone's expense. Our relationship was based on humor, but it went much deeper than that. Underneath the humor, Dave was very serious about his family, church, many friends, and business. Even serious conversations took on a humorous twist. Dave is one of those unique characters who also has character. He is a joy to be around.

## Humility

Being humble can be an endearing quality, especially when the alternative is an egotist or narcissist. Given a choice, I will always choose to be with the humble person. A humble person is usually respectful and courteous to others. He or she is open to other peoples' ideas, recognizing they do not have all the answers.

A senior partner in a large, international law firm, Bob ranks among the very best attorneys in America. He has developed a specialty within his legal practice, which has placed his talents and services in great demand. A top graduate of a highly respected school of business and one of the best law schools in the country, Bob's academic credentials are impeccable. He counsels many of the biggest medical technology firms in the world and has received numerous accolades for his legal abilities.

Bob doesn't blow his own horn. He is hesitant to talk about his accomplishments. He would rather steer the conversation toward someone else. He is a better listener than a talker. Bob exudes character.

## Honesty

George Washington "could not tell a lie." Abraham Lincoln was known as "Honest Abe." Both George and Abe are highly respected presidents, due in large part to their reputation for honesty. To them, honesty was a virtue—a quality to be pursued.

Times have changed in American politics. Truth and honesty have become casualties of the partisanship, bickering, and blaming that knows no bounds in Washington.

Honesty builds character. It is not always easy to be honest. Sometimes the truth is downright painful and inconvenient. Jan and I see the honesty challenge in our real estate business when a seller is hesitant to disclose a less than obvious defect in the home to a buyer. Our role as Realtors is to make sure there is proper disclosure, resulting in both seller and buyer feeling good about themselves and the transaction.

## Helpfulness

Everyone needs a helping hand from time to time. It is human nature to find ourselves in occasional (or frequent) trouble. We rely on each other to meet some of the challenges of life. People who willingly and unconditionally help their fellow human beings are overflowing with character. We see willing helpers in all walks of life, but especially in such helping professions as teaching, nursing, and mental health.

Bill had a serious drinking problem as a young adult. Alcohol was destroying his health, career, and family relationships. When he hit bottom, his family was there for him. With his family's help, Bill embarked on the long road to recovery from alcoholism. He's been sober for over forty years and has led a successful, productive life.

In the past forty years Bill has invited many problem drinkers to attend Alcoholic Anonymous meetings with him, to begin their own recoveries from this dreaded disease. Help has come full circle. Helping others continues to strengthen Bill's recovery process. He is constantly paying forward the help he received as a young man.

During the writing of this book, Jan and I were in the eye of the biggest hurricane to hit Florida in recorded history. Hurricane Irma moved up from Key West to Marco Island to Naples and Bonita Springs on its path of destruction throughout the Sunshine State. We hunkered down in our shuttered home and felt the storm's wrath. When the storm finally passed, lack of electricity, damaged homes, downed trees, and serious flooding remained. The recovery outlook was overwhelming. Neighbors soon began helping neighbors: those with power shared their homes with residents without power; dwindling supplies of food, water, and ice were freely shared; and when traveling became a possibility, brigades of helpers arrived from all over the country.

Our neighbors hosted a group of young men with chain saws that drove down from the Tampa area. They brought their own gasoline to power the chain saws, as gas was not readily available in our ravaged area following the hurricane. This group of young men moved from house to house in our community, cutting downed trees into small pieces that could be hauled to the street for ultimate pickup by the county. Grateful homeowners offered them compensation for their efforts, but they refused to be paid for their volunteer work. It was their mission to help others in a time of great need. We don't even know their names, but I am absolutely sure that every one of them has character.

Withdrawals from the character account:

People who hate have a deep emotional dislike for another person or group. Hate mongers are a scourge on civilized society. They tend to see the world in terms of them versus us. We have seen hatred demonstrated at the highest political level, with some politicians identifying normal people and the free press as "enemies of the state" simply because they do not agree with someone else's behavior, words, or policies.

Hate mongers are sad, angry people who try to project their anger and sadness onto others. Hate-filled people have a bankrupt character account.

Arrogant, conceited people who are caught up with their own self-importance have contracted the dreaded disease of hubris. It is a condition that often leads to a person's downfall, draining the character account along the way.

Hypocrites pretend to have high moral standards, but their words and deeds don't match their pretenses. Hypocrisy is most visible in the political world, where directly opposite positions are taken depending on the political situation. Often, hypocrites condemn another person for the exact behavior they themselves have exercised in the past—and may again in the future. High standards and moral positions are abandoned in favor of an expedient outcome.

**Questions to consider:**

Do I maintain a sense of humor through serious times?

Is it all about me in my daily conversations?

Am I totally honest even when the truth hurts?

How do I react to hypocritical behavior?

Am I ever hypocritical?

# Chapter I

> What if strong moral stands
> Are taken in the face of demands?
> Would we grow in esteem and value
> For the right things that we do?
> JB

Deposits into the character account:

## Integrity

People of integrity have nothing to hide. They have strong moral beliefs and tend to live lives based on values, principles, and a consistency of righteous actions. A person of integrity follows a consistent path for making decisions so that other people know that he or she will be measured, sane, and sensible, no matter the situation. Values will always prevail. Such people can be considered "true north," and their character account is overflowing.

I was privileged to serve on several not-for-profit committees with Paul, who was retired from a long and successful career as chief legal counsel, first for North American Van Lines and later for Pepsico. Paul spent his retirement years helping others, primarily by serving charitable organizations. He and his wife eventually left their considerable estate to a charitable foundation.

Paul's BS meter was set on high, and he very quickly and fully grasped situations and understood what needed to happen. He had little tolerance for dealing with people whose compass was pointing in another direction. Paul was nice, polite, and direct in his communications. His role was not to embarrass others but to teach them a better way. His integrity showed through his words and his actions. I always knew where Paul was coming from, and I marveled at his ability to find solutions to problems that were win–win solutions. Paul epitomizes integrity for me.

## Inner Peace

Persons with integrity are far more likely to enjoy inner peace. Peace of mind in a busy, hectic, stressful world is not always an easy task. Inner peace is an important ingredient for building character. It is only possible if we consistently do the right thing. Having our thoughts, words, and actions in alignment can lead to feeling at peace; it is a prerequisite for promoting peace in the world. We cannot give what we don't have.

There are many paths to inner peace and many teachers available to show us the way. Whatever the path, choosing peace is ultimately a personal choice. Some people are addicted to stress and choose turmoil or conflict over peace. In my experience, stress erodes character; inner peace nurtures character.

## Intention

There is an old saying: "The path to hell is paved with good intentions." Those are not the kind of intentions that build character. To me, intention denotes a purpose, a plan, a mind-set. It is much more than a wish. Intention is the fuel that allows us to achieve our goals. It involves intentionality.

Sometimes we think about various paths to take, considering first one and then another. It is only when we make the conscious decision, intending to pursue a particular path or plan that things start to happen. It creates a strengthened commitment within our minds.

When I journal early each morning, thinking about my day, I tend to avoid terms like "plan" or "wish." Rather, I form intentions for the day: "I intend to bike forty miles this morning"; "I intend to write from 1:00 p.m. to 4:00 p.m."; or "I intend to maintain my inner peace, no matter what happens today." Framing my life with intentions tends to create the energy I need to live each day to the fullest.

## Introspection

Psychologically, we are all built differently. Some of us are extroverts; some of us are introverts; and many of us are somewhere on the scale in between the extremes. Where we are on the scale can change from situation to situation, moment to moment, or over years. There is no right or wrong way to be, as long as we are being true to our own nature.

Whether we are an introvert or an extrovert, it is a good thing to be able to look inside. Being aware of our own mental or emotional state can help all of us to understand our effect on ourselves and the world around us. We can learn to fully utilize our natural talents and also strengthen hidden talents that enable us to evolve into well-adjusted, fully functioning, confident individuals.

## Inspiration

When we are mentally stimulated and our creative juices are flowing, I believe it is more than a mental process. When I am inspired, I feel like I am connected with my spiritual side. It feels like I have a direct connection with the divine, allowing me to stretch beyond my own physical, mental, and emotional borders.

Writing is an arena for inspiration for me. I can be struggling with a topic, and all of a sudden a way forward is presented to me. I often wonder, Where did that come from? Athletes experience this connection when they are in the flow of peak performance. For most of us inspiration is not an everyday experience, but we do know what it feels like. Certain daily practices such as prayer or meditation can sometimes promote inspiration in our lives. Fear, anger, and stress usually limit our moments of inspiration.

Withdrawals from the character account:

Isolating ourselves from the world may seem enticing when life becomes too hectic or stressful. It may even be a good thing to take a break and be alone from time to time. However, human contact and relationships are important ingredients for personal growth and development. Totally withdrawing into one's self is rarely a good option for most people.

Isolationism as a nation periodically rears its head in America. There are those who would prefer that America build a wall around its perimeter, withdraw its membership in the United Nations and other international organizations, and keep outside influences and foreigners from entering into our country. In my opinion, isolationism is an excellent way to stunt the character of our great nation.

Living in a consistent state of irritation destroys inner peace and joy. Being irritable is a choice we make. We are always free to choose peace instead. Some people spend their lives feeling irritated at every little thing. It is like an automatic reaction, justifying their anger at the world. Irritable people fail to see the many blessings of life and consistently withdraw from their dwindling character account.

**Questions to consider:**

Which is more important to me: being right or feeling peaceful inside?

Am I a true north person occasionally, when it is convenient; usually; or always, even when there is a price to pay?

What does it feel like to be inspired?

Am I irritable too much of the time?

# Chapter J

What if life seems unfair,
At times feeling too much to bear?
Know a new day will dawn
And life will go on,
As long as we refuse to despair.
JB

Deposits into the character account:

## Justice

It is true. Life is sometimes beyond our control and not always fair. Sometimes justice is nowhere in sight. The things we can control include the ways we react to injustice and treat other people. The choices we make will determine the impact of an injustice on our character account.

When a delusional young man steeped in messages of hatred and racism killed a group of innocent church members in Charleston, South Carolina, it wasn't fair to the victims or their families. However, their reaction after the incident, to love and forgive the killer, was a choice to empower and free themselves from the bondages of hate. Those grieving families chose to replenish their character accounts.

Justice is being tested in many ways around the world. Terrorist actions committed in the name of religion are claiming victims on a regular basis. Senseless murders, sometimes committed by law enforcement officials on minority groups, reek of injustice. Natural disasters such as hurricanes, floods, wildfires, and earthquakes inflict untold misery on vast populations. Life can be unfair. It is the way we choose to react that can make all the difference.

Treating other people justly is also a personal decision. Having a sense of fair play is essential to building a character account. We have an inner sense of knowing if we are dispensing justice or exploiting a person or a situation for our own benefit at the expense of someone else.

## Joy

To be joyful is also an individual choice. Different people react to situations in differing ways. Feelings of pleasure and happiness are absorbed more easily by some people than others. An identical situation can be seen as good fortune by one person and disappointing to someone else. I've known people to grouse and complain in the face of what I perceive to be great news. Joy does not come easily to some people.

Claudette was a recovering nun who had gone to ministerial school after leaving the convent. I met Claudette when she was the minister of Unity Church in Fort Wayne. Joy radiated from Claudette in good times and in difficult challenges, and her joy was contagious. She saw God's hand in every situation, including her own cancer, which brought her life to a premature conclusion. Claudette chose to appreciate life, including its end phase. Sharing her joy was part of her mission on earth.

## Judgment

Having good judgment (common sense) is different from judging others. Behaving appropriately and making good choices is an important building block for character. Good judgment is an essential part of having integrity. Acting stupid, failing to take responsibility for our actions, and harming ourselves or other people unnecessarily are ways of depleting our character account. They might make us characters but not characters with character.

When we act responsibly, doing the appropriate thing, other people understand that they can rely on our judgment. Our personal power and influence grow, including our own self-esteem. It is a win–win situation whenever we exercise good judgment.

Withdrawals from the character account:

When we judge another person, we identify ourselves as a person who judges. It might feel good temporarily to call another person a derogative name or accuse them of being a bad person. It seems to be human nature to want to lift ourselves up by putting someone else down. The psychological term for slamming others is projection. We think that we can cast out our own sense of inadequacy by drawing attention to the inadequacy in another. Judging is a temporary fix that usually comes back in the end to bite the one who judges.

Being an obnoxious, contemptible jerk is not behavior that promotes character building. This type of behavior is revealing of a personality that is insecure.

When we are jealous of someone else's success or good fortune, we are demonstrating resentment, bitterness, and mistrust. Jealousy is a character flaw that erodes character.

## Questions to consider:

Who are the people in my life who exude joy?

Do I have a highly developed sense of justice?

Do I sometimes judge or label other people?

Am I jealous when someone close to me is successful?

# Chapter K

What if we choose to be kind
To that person who's falling behind?
A small helping hand
Makes a difference and
Strengthens our own peace of mind.
JB

Deposits into the character account:

## Kindness

When we are friendly, generous, helpful, and considerate of another person, the value of an act of kindness cannot be underestimated—both for the receiver and the giver. Kindness has the power to change a culture.

Joseph and Mary celebrate Random Acts of Kindness Day 365 days of the year. Sometimes they help someone they know; sometimes it is a total stranger; sometimes the recipient of their kindness is a rescued pet. Their mission is to spread acts of kindness everywhere and to everyone, with faith that kindness will be paid forward by the recipients. It's a bit like Johnny Appleseed, the legendary folk hero who introduced apple trees to much of North America. Joseph and Mary plant their seeds of kindness, knowing that the seeds will grow and scatter in the wind.

## Knowledge

There is an old saying: "Knowledge is power." Knowledge can be acquired through experience, education, or training. Some people seem to have an innate command of knowledge. However it is acquired, knowledge is an important aspect of a civilized world.

In today's world it is impossible for any one person to acquire a depth of knowledge in all subjects. We live in a complex world, and it needs knowledgeable people in every vital phase. People with knowledge work together to keep the lights on, airplanes flying, motor vehicles moving, food production going, technology advancing, governments functioning—the list is endless. A multitude of areas of knowledge are required to operate the system. Every person has a role.

Teaching is an undervalued profession in America that has created a system for sharing and passing along information and knowledge from generation to generation, always expanding and growing the base of knowledge. From nursery schools to universities and beyond, the constant search for knowledge has spurred civilized nations to develop.

Personal knowledge and expertise allow individuals to be productive members of a knowledge-based society. Participation in the process is character building.

## Karma

Hindus, Buddhists, and many others believe in the concept of karma. It can be described as "What goes around comes around." I like to think that it simply means that giving and receiving are the same. If we want to be aware of how we are treating others, we need only look at the way we are being treated. Sooner or later, we receive back what we give.

Having a karmic awareness helps us to become better people, improving the way we treat others. As we become kinder and nicer, we find ourselves being treated with kindness and respect. Our self-esteem grows, and we develop character. It is a vicious circle, and it is important that we move through life at a high level of the circle.

### Keys

Understanding the keys to unlocking the complexities of life is an important element of a successful experience. Many people go through their entire lives without a clue as to what makes them happy or successful. People who learn the keys that work for them have a giant advantage over the rest of humankind. Being open, curious, and introspective may be just the keys for discovering the secrets to success.

Withdrawals from the character account:

To keen is to lament, wail, or cry. Sometimes it is important to grieve or mourn a loss. It is an important step in a recovery process. Too often, however, we see people lamenting or bemoaning situations that call for energy, focus, and toughness in resolving the issue. Keening inappropriately can empty a character account.

A knave is a dishonest or unscrupulous person who takes advantage of other people. It is a disparaging description for a villain or scoundrel. Acting like a knave is a drain on character.

When we knuckle under to peer pressure or misguided authority, we submit or give up our own moral compass in exchange for accepting someone else's power. Ceding our personal power is usually not a good way to build character.

## Questions to consider:

Do I practice random acts of kindness in my daily life?

Do I actively pursue knowledge in order to expand my horizons?

What are the keys for living up to my potential?

Am I a whiner/complainer?

## Chapter L

> What if we love one another,
> Be we friends, enemies, or strangers?
> The power created by love
> Can make each one of us life changers.
> JB

Deposits into the character account:

## LOVE

According to the Principles of Attitudinal Healing, the essence of our being is love. When we are unloving, we are acting out of fear and giving a call for help. The concept of love extends far beyond a romantic or sexual relationship. It is a state of consciousness that governs relationships with partners, family members, friends, pets, objects, and activities. Love is an underlying emotion that emanates from the essence of our being. It transcends fears.

When we are in the presence of a person who emanates unconditional love, we feel the joy all around us; not a trace of fear is in the air. My golf buddy, Joe, is such a person of love. A retired schoolteacher, Joe just goes with the flow, without judging, condemning, whining, or complaining. He goes out of his way to be helpful to everyone around him. He deeply cares about everyone in his life—even those who sometimes make life difficult for him.

Most religions promote love as the ideal but define love with conditions. It is acceptable to love people who agree with us but not the "infidels" who have a different dogma. In my opinion, this is not a true form of love. It fails to perceive the essence of love in anyone with a different point of view.

## Light

*Light* is one of those words with multiple meanings. As a noun, it can mean a lamp or illumination or understanding; as a verb it can mean to ignite something, like a fire or an emotion; as an adjective it can describe a color or a room or the weight of an object.

Relating to character, light involves an emotional state. People who can retain a light disposition in the face of stressful or dangerous forces have an advantage over the rest of us. It is a talent to feel lighthearted when everyone around us is fearful and deadly serious.

Certain athletes have the innate ability to remain cool and collected during crunch time. Michael Jordan was one of those gifted athletes; he had the "just give me the ball" mentality when a nervous fear was present. Jordan Spieth can joke with his caddy as he prepares to hit the shot that will determine if he will win or lose the golf tournament. Learning to feel loose and light, even in serious situations, builds character.

## Leadership

Dr. Stephen Covey wrote a best-seller entitled *Principle-Centered Leadership*. I have read and reread his book several times, trying to absorb the leadership principles espoused.

He bases principle-centered leadership on what he describes as being "true north." These leaders live in harmony with fairness, equity, justice, integrity, honesty, and trust. They are not into using their power to control other people or gain sexual favors. Their focus is being of service.

During my years in the practice of law, I experienced interactions with large law firms, businesses, social groups, and religious and charitable organizations. I observed firsthand various forms of leadership. Having studied Dr. Covey's treatise on effective leadership, it was interesting for me to become aware of the leadership style and characteristics of these organizations.

Rob was CEO of a large foundation that provided funding for promising charitable organizations all over the world. The foundation's concept was to provide seed money to get an organization up and running, but it was careful not to allow the charity to become dependent on the foundation for funding for the indefinite future. In the interim, the foundation provided workshops and seminars to assist the management of its recipient organizations. Depending on the circumstances, funding was usually provided for two to three years; after this time, the organization was expected to be self-sufficient. I served on the board of one of the foundation's recipients, and it felt like tough love when the funding stopped.

Rob was loved and respected by his staff, his board of directors, and the boards of recipient charitable organizations. Everyone knew what to expect, and Rob openly communicated with all interested parties. He was helpful when help was needed; he was tough but fair when it was time to leave the nest. Rob was a role model for developing character.

## Learning

Life is one long learning process. We learn from formal education, training, mentoring, teaching, and, most of all, experience. We learn from our elders, our children, our grandchildren, our friends, and perfect strangers. Learning and personal growth are compatible. The quality of our learning is dependent on a willingness to be open, an ability to learn from experience, a drive to pursue education and training, and a willingness to listen. Intellectual curiosity is a gift that is exploited by learned people. People who already "know it all" actually know very little. Avid learners tend to have character.

## Liberal

Like the conservative label, being liberal was a personality trait long before it became a political label. The term *liberal* refers to being generous, flexible, open to new ideas, tolerant, and charitable. The political pundits have hijacked the term to refer to people who are left of center on the political spectrum.

Liberal education usually means an approach that emphasizes our general knowledge and experience, compared with an educational approach that is more technical or training oriented. Even for someone who identifies as a political conservative, having liberal personality traits can build character.

## Laughter

It is true that laughter can be the best medicine. It can reduce the level of stress we feel in our busy lives, and laughter can trigger the release of endorphins that promote a sense of well-being. Laughter also has the ability to decrease pain and improve job performance. Most people are attracted to individuals who have the contagious ability to laugh and to cause us to laugh with them.

## Legacy

Everyone who has ever lived has left some form of legacy behind. That legacy might be money, buildings, careers, good works, paintings, books, or simply memories for the people who loved or hated us. We are all just passing through life, and we will eventually leave this world with nothing but a legacy.

Hitler's legacy was a war-torn planet and relentless persecution of those groups of people he regarded as inferior. Mother Teresa's legacy was the gratitude of the poor and suffering who were helped by her acts of kindness. My dad's legacy was our remembrance of his generosity, kindnesses, and integrity. That legacy trumps the inheritance of money that he left his family.

Withdrawals from the character account:

Lying can be an occasional thing or it can be pathological. The inability to trust that a person who is speaking is telling the truth can lead to serious adverse consequences. Lies can be outright or half-truths. Either form of lying is a problem. America is witnessing the consequences of lying at the highest level of politics. Trust in government is sinking to all-time lows as many of the lies become apparent. Liars are a plague on society and erode the character of our culture.

Being lazy, lethargic, and unproductive is not an avenue to building a character account. Maintaining a healthy balance between work, play, and rest can be an important characteristic for adding to character. We live on a planet that is constantly in motion. Moving ourselves is usually a good idea.

Loathing someone means that we hate that person with a passion. It is an intense dislike or aversion to the person. Hate and loathing are dangerous emotions that can be destructive of our own well-being, not to mention the well-being of the person being loathed.

A belief in limitations is counterproductive. There are no limits to human potential. Our only limitations are based on our limited thinking or believing. Our thinking determines our reality.

**Questions to consider:**

Do I think of myself as a leader or a follower?

Is my love for other people unconditional?

What am I learning about myself right now?

What will be my legacy?

Am I living up to my full potential?

# Chapter M

*What if our vision is blurred,*
*With no clear path for our life?*
*With no direction inferred,*
*Life can fill with turmoil and strife.*
JB

Deposits into the character account:

# Mission

Every person on earth has a mission, whether it is conscious or not. Missions can become fuzzy or confusing at times, as life presents its twists and turns. Being aware of our mission is a large step in the direction of leading a productive, meaningful life.

Successful organizations develop clear mission statements. Successful people do likewise. A mission statement identifies our purpose for being here, our goals, and our strategies for reaching our goals. Going through life without an awareness of our mission is like traveling without a road map, compass, or GPS. We have no idea where we are, where we are going, or who we want to be. Our mission can be an evolving, changing, living statement as we move through the life process.

My college roommate, Chuck, is the son of a school principal. Chuck knew from an early age that his mission in life was to be an educator. Chuck diligently followed his path. After obtaining his educational credentials, he began teaching; he then followed the path of becoming an assistant principal, the principal of a high school, and the superintendent of schools. There were obstacles and challenges along the way, but Chuck knew where he was, where he wanted to go, and how to get there. He was determined to make a difference in the educational system. Chuck's depth of character was evident as early as his college years, and it has not faded in the passing decades.

## Modeling

Role models play an important job in American culture. Every one of us is modeling something every waking moment that we are with another person. People tend to emulate the behavior of the people around them.

I have been blessed with a constant flow of excellent role models: my parents, siblings, teachers, fellow students, partners, clients, friends, spouse, and children. In contrast, I have observed the role modeling that is sometimes available to gang members, criminals, convicts in prison, victims of abuse, and addicts. We are heavily influenced by the behavior modeled in our circumstances, good or bad. It takes a strong character to break free of poor role models; it takes a weak character to ignore the influences of excellent role models.

## Morality

*Morality* is generally defined as a system of values and principles of conduct of a person or society. It does not always mean the same thing to everyone. No system of morality is universal, as cultures and standards vary. Morality involves the distinction between right and wrong within the particular society.

In one society it may be moral and ethical to commit a terrorist act against an infidel. In another, it may be considered moral and appropriate to deny rights to a person because of gender or religious beliefs. Different cultures and civilizations develop different codes of conduct.

Many Americans firmly believe that the American moral standards are the "right" one, and that everyone else in the world should adopt our belief system. I am not so sure about that, especially considering recent revelations of the moral standards of people in powerful positions in government, business, education, entertainment, and religion. Perhaps America too is still a work in process with regard to moral values.

## Motivation

Motivation is the desire or willingness to do something, to take action. It requires enthusiasm, energy, drive, consistency, and determination. Being motivated is a necessary element for leading a productive life.

Some people are self-motivated, initiating action on their own. Other people require an external force, such as a boss or financial carrot, to be motivated. Whatever the source, motivated people are the wheels that keep our system moving and growing.

## Meditation

Meditation is a mental exercise that trains the mind, similar to the way physical fitness trains the body. When I meditate, my mind quiets down and relaxes. It helps me to focus on the here and now of my life. I like to think of meditation as the flip side of prayer. Prayer is how we talk to God; meditation is how we listen to God.

There are many forms of meditation that are oriented to specific goals. It can be connected with the practice of yoga; its goal can be mindfulness; it can be used to alleviate physical pain. Whatever form it takes, quieting the mind can be an effective tool for functioning at a higher level and building character.

## Magnanimous

To be magnanimous is to have a generous spirit. Specifically, it means to be extremely forgiving and generous toward a rival or more vulnerable person. Powerful elected officials who use their position of power to prosecute and victimize their vanquished opponents are not acting magnanimously. Sports teams who "run up the score" against an inferior team are not magnanimous. Interestingly, karma often rears its ugly head in the form of payback when the shoe is on the other foot.

## Mentoring

A few successful individuals make the special effort to mentor someone, forming a special, long-term relationship focused on the growth and development of the person being mentored. A mentor is a source of wisdom who guides a less experienced, less knowledgeable person.

Tom has spent his entire career in the field of mental health counseling and has developed a well-earned reputation as a wise counselor. As he moves through his seventies, Tom is using his knowledge and expertise to mentor students in the Masters level program for mental health counselors. He is helping these young students to transition from book learning to actual experience in the field. Tom's character is being shared and increased.

Withdrawals from the character account:

Being mean-spirited, making a conscious effort to harm or defame another person, is an indication that the ego is in charge. Mean-spirited people see other people as their enemy, rather than as a brother or sister who is a fellow passenger on this journey called life. They love to see other people fail. Their cruel, unkind behavior is intended to be hurtful.

Being around mean-spirited people makes me feel sad. I observe their personal misery because they are the real losers in the process. It is particularly painful to see mean-spirited people at the highest levels of government. Their character accounts are running on empty.

*Myopic* refers to a condition of the eye: being near-sighted. It can also refer to a short-sighted person who lacks imagination or vision. A narrow-minded individual is often described as myopic, lacking a vision of the big picture. Myopic people usually lack character as well.

To be Machiavellian is to be unscrupulous, deceptive, or manipulative. The term is named after an Italian diplomat of the fifteenth century who is considered the father of modern political science. Political expediency trumps morality and uses cunning and deceit to carry out the agenda of the ruling party. Some things never change!

## Questions to consider:

What is my personal mission?

Who are my role models?

What kind of role model am I?

Am I a self-motivated person?

## Chapter N

> What if each stranger we meet
> Is viewed as a neighbor and friend?
> Would it affect how we greet
> Everyone on the street,
> Might there be no need to offend?
> JB

Deposits into character account:

## Neighbors

Being neighborly is a lost art in many urban settings. We tend to be focused on our own family, work, and social organizations, without really getting to know our neighbors. Sometimes it takes a disaster to bring us together.

For some of us in Southwest Florida, Hurricane Irma was just such a disaster. It was amazing to watch neighbors spring into action to help each other. The lucky home owners with power hosted the neighbors whose homes remained without electricity for more than a week after the storm; limited supplies of food, water, and ice were shared freely; and neighbors helped neighbors to clean up the debris left behind. When grocery stores reopened using generators, neighbors with vehicles able to drive through flooded streets brought groceries back to the home-bound; rakes, shovels, and other tools were shared in the cleanup process; and a new bond was formed in the neighborhood. Being a good neighbor is an excellent way to contribute to a character account.

## Nice

Personally, I think that being a nice person is an undervalued quality. For most of us, it does not take a lot of energy to be pleasant, agreeable, and friendly. Being nice can make a huge difference in the life of someone else.

Our society has some attitudes about nice: "Nice guys finish last" or "She's a nice person, but ..." Maybe it is time for us to reconsider the value of being nice. Maybe there would be less anger, bitterness, and violence in the world if we treated each other with civility, courtesy, and consideration. Being nice is an easy way to build up a character account.

## Nurturing

Relationships need to be nurtured in order to flourish. Most plants require nurturing in order to grow. Children need nurturing in order to develop. Nurturing involves providing encouragement, care, and support. We also need to nurture ourselves. We can't give away something that we don't have within us.

Nurturing comes easily for some people; for others it is a learned way of being. Whether it comes naturally or not, being nurturing is a valuable trait for building character.

Amy has a background in social work. Most close family and friends refer to her as "Saint Amy"; a few humorously refer to her as "Crazy Amy." She and her husband have lovingly raised a special-needs child, who has lived well beyond her life expectancy because of her parents' nurturing. They have also raised a biological daughter, adopted a toddler from an orphanage in China, and adopted a foster son. Amy's nurturing knows no limits, and her character account is overflowing.

## Nonjudgment

When I judge another person, I do not define the person being judged; rather, I define myself as someone who judges other people. Many of us have been conditioned to make judgments about others, and we need to learn nonjudgment. The more we judge others, the more we tend to judge ourselves.

It is important to become aware of how our minds are constantly judging and then step back and think about the judgments we are making. Is there another way to see the behavior or circumstances being judged? What would it be like to accept or forgive the behavior? What does our ego get out of voicing the judgment? Judging others is not a way to build a character account.

Judging and evaluating are not synonymous terms. When we evaluate a person in a leadership role, we are assessing how well the person is performing as a leader so that we can determine if we want to retain or oust that leader. Evaluation is an important step in holding our leaders accountable for their actions. When we form an opinion on the value of a product or service, we are assessing its worth in order to make a decision. Evaluation is a necessary ingredient of everyday life. Judging other people is not.

## Noble

People of noble character have lofty ideals. Used in this way, it does not mean aristocratic or blue-blooded. Rather, noble people have developed outstanding minds and maintain high moral standards. Every one of us has the option to be of noble character, no matter our family of origin, circumstances, or lifestyle. Having lofty ideals is a pathway to character.

## No Limits

Dr. Wayne Dyer taught us that there are no limits to who we can be and what we can achieve. We are all capable of transcending our self-perceived limits. People with no limits often see themselves as spiritual beings first and human beings second. They do not feel bound by human norms and expectations.

Dr. Dyer himself was an example of a person without limits. Raised by a single parent, under conditions that most people would consider extremely limiting, Dr. Dyer worked his way through the educational system in starts and stops, twists and turns. He eventually received a PhD in psychology. He practiced therapy for many years and began writing books about his no-limit philosophy. Many of his books became best sellers and remain valuable resources for the rest of us, even after his death. He is still showing us the way to go beyond our self-perceived limits.

Withdrawals from the character account:

Narrow-mindedness is a social disease. It is an unwillingness to consider other points of view. People who are narrow-minded usually have limited perspectives and tend to be bigoted, intolerant, and self-righteous. This condition is detrimental to building character.

Some people I have known seem to take personal pleasure in being nasty. It connotes a lack of courtesy, caring, or kindness. Nasty people are inevitably sad and angry. Being nasty is not a pleasant way to live, and I do my best to avoid nasty behavior.

Maintaining a negative attitude is a personal choice. It is a habitual, automatic way of seeing that the glass is half empty. A pessimist always expects the worst and is rarely disappointed. Negative people often compare themselves unfavorably with others. Chronic negative attitudes can adversely affect our health, happiness, and well-being.

A namby-pamby person is weak and indecisive. There is no clear purpose in his or her life, and the true north compass points in many directions. Such people are considered to be lacking in character.

Narcissists tend to manipulate and exploit other people for their own needs. They lack emotional empathy and feel entitled to abuse others. Cruelty is a pattern of the narcissistic personality. They have an inflated sense of self-importance, often with a deep need for admiration. Narcissistic leaders are vulnerable to being played by political foes and foreign leaders who are willing to compliment them and pretend to be impressed with their powers.

## Questions to consider:

Am I a good neighbor?

Do I judge other people on the basis of their physical appearance, financial status, or level of education?

What limits have I imposed on my own development as a person?

Do I have a nasty streak that needs to get out from time to time? If so, how do I feel about it?

## Chapter O

> What if we looked at problems
> As lessons from the school of hard knocks?
> Answers can be found
> If we just look around
> For solutions outside the box.
> JB

Deposits to the character account:

## Outside the Box

Sometimes situations appear to be insurmountable. There is no obvious solution to the problem. This is when the person of character is willing to think outside the box to find a solution. This means an ability to think differently, unconventionally, from a new perspective.

When Thomas Edison struggled to invent the electric light bulb, the conventional wisdom was that it was time to cut his losses and move on to something else. Mr. Edison chose to see the situation differently: he ended up trying about ten thousand ways *not* to make a light bulb. He learned from every failure and continued to experiment with new ideas until he succeeded.

In business, standard operating procedures create a structure around the box of ways to think about solutions. Complex problems sometimes require creativity and innovative ideas that do not represent standard operating procedure. Getting out of the box involves shifting the perspective and a willingness to try new ways. People who are willing to think outside the box are often persons of character.

## Open-Mindedness

An element of thinking outside the box is a willingness to be open-minded. No one has all the answers. No one is right all the time. We can learn from each other if our minds are open to new thoughts and ideas.

To be open-minded means to be unbiased, unprejudiced, willing to give many different opinions careful consideration. It involves a willingness to change our mind if a new suggestion makes more sense than our previous opinion. Open-mindedness would do wonders for the collective character of the United States Congress, not to mention American citizens.

## Optimism

Optimists are generally confident and hopeful about the future. They expect a favorable outcome in any situation and possess a light, happy mental attitude. Positive emotions can be self-fulfilling. We tend to get what we expect out of life. If we expect the worst, we are usually right on.

Being optimistic is a choice. We choose our thoughts, so why not choose happy, hopeful, positive thoughts? Channeling our thoughts toward a positive, happy goal can be an effective way to deal with depression. Studies indicate that people who maintain a positive mind-set are healthier in the long run than people who focus on the negative. They are also a lot more pleasant to be around.

## Overcoming

To overcome is to deal effectively with a problem, difficulty, or challenge. People who prevail over adversity become stronger for the experience. Several US government leaders were born into poverty or difficult family circumstances and managed to nevertheless prevail and go on to graduate from Ivy League schools and succeed in politics. They tend to have a better grasp of peoples' problems as a result of their own challenging experiences.

Min-jun and Seo-yeon moved from South Korea to Ohio, following Min-jun's graduation from medical school in Korea. He did his residency in Ohio, even though he spoke very little English and Seo-yeon spoke almost no English. They lived in a small one-bedroom apartment with very little furniture. It was a lonely time for Seo-yeon, as it was difficult to make friends without speaking the native language. Min-jun picked up English fairly quickly in his work at the hospital.

Eventually this Korean couple moved to a small town in the Midwest, where Min-jun practiced psychiatric medicine. Their two daughters were born in that small town. Over the decades, while maintaining family ties and friendships in South Korea, they acclimated to American ways and became American citizens. Both are now excellent golfers (Seo-yeon has been women's club champion at their country club on numerous occasions), and they are active members of their community. They prevailed over very difficult circumstances and came out stronger together. Today their two daughters are both happily married dentists and have provided their proud parents with grandsons. The amount of character in that family is overwhelming.

## Objectivity

A truly objective person (or news organization) strives to reduce or eliminate biases and prejudices, relying only on verifiable facts and data. It means a position of neutrality and impartiality in forming opinions.

A national news network promotes itself as being "fair and balanced." From my perspective, there is a sad lacking of objectivity in how they present the news. Opinions pass through their biased filter and come out slanted. To me it seems like more of a propaganda machine than a news network. In my opinion the network often lacks objectivity.

Withdrawals from the character account:

We have all experienced obnoxious behavior from time to time. Perhaps we have even been guilty of acting obnoxiously ourselves. It is extremely unpleasant to be around obnoxious behavior, and it feels even worse when we are the one who is obnoxious. It can wipe out a character account in a New York minute.

Obscene behavior may involve sexually explicit, indecent, smutty pornography. Recent news has featured obscene behavior in sexual assault and/or sexual harassment cases that have caused powerful icons to topple. It can also refer to any other shocking, frightful, inappropriate behavior that is repugnant to moral principles. Acting obscenely is not a way to build character.

Obstreperous behavior is often found in childhood, and most people grow out of it in time. It is an angry, defiant, inappropriately aggressive form of behavior that is very unpleasant to be around. Being obstreperous is not a positive trait, especially for an adult.

**Questions to consider:**

Do I think of myself as a rigid thinker, or am I an open-minded person?

Where do I stand on the scale between being negative and being positive?

What are some of the major challenges I have overcome so far in my life?

How do I react to obnoxious or obscene behavior?

# Chapter P

*What if my own inner peace*
*Is contagious, just like a disease?*
*We spread what's inside*
*To all we confide,*
*Like germs afloat on the breeze.*
*JB*

Deposits into the character account:

## Peaceful

When minds are tranquil and free of fear, inner peace has room to grow and develop. Peace of mind is a personal choice, dependent on the thoughts we select. Our suffering or happiness evolves from within. Calm, quiet, serene individuals exude inner strength. We enjoy being in their presence, and we try to absorb their energy.

Jack was a commercial lending officer at a bank in Fort Wayne. He had an uncanny ability to determine credit worthiness of a business person, based not only on financial numbers but also on the character of the person applying for a loan. His own inner peace influenced many of his customers, and they worked overtime to repay the loans because they did not want to disappoint Jack.

Jack maintained the attitude that the person was more important than the money. He refused to be fearful, and quietly accepted whatever circumstances arose with his customers. If economic conditions made business success difficult, he chose to work with his customers to find a graceful solution. Over the decades, some of Jack's failed business customers later became his biggest success stories. Jack's sense of inner peace was a great source of his character.

### Powerful

Like inner peace, personal power is a consequence, a by-product of living a character-based life. Inner peace and personal power are partners in the character building process. Personal power has nothing to do with being forceful or dominating other people; rather, it is an aura of influence that creates natural leaders. In James Allen's classic book, *As a Man Thinketh*, he indicates that the more tranquil we become, the greater our success, influence, and power for good.

America is sometimes described as the greatest power on earth. I believe that is true, not because we have the world's largest nuclear arsenal or the most destructive weapons or the best trained warriors. I believe it is true because of the many freedom-loving Americans who work every day to do the right thing, help others, and grow their character accounts.

### Perseverance

A persevering character is steadfast in the face of difficulties. Perseverance involves tenacity, a determination to succeed no matter the obstacles or delays. Perseverance requires an inner toughness that simply won't give up. Having a clear sense of purpose is a necessity to persevere.

Sue graduated from Purdue University with a degree in industrial engineering, a profession historically dominated by men. While married and raising two daughters, Sue formed her own consulting business and traveled all over North America, helping companies with creative problem solving. Later, with her daughters in tow, she commuted from her home in Evansville to the University of Louisville to obtain her PhD. She dropped off her daughters at her parents' home halfway in between Evansville and Louisville, and she then picked them up on her way home after class. With her doctorate in hand, Sue founded the Center for Applied Research at the University of Southern Indiana and ventured into the world of politics. After three years as Indiana's lieutenant governor, Sue was selected as the president of Indiana Vocational and Technical College (IVY Tech), the largest state college in Indiana, with campuses all over the state and nearly one hundred thousand students.

Sue is a case study in perseverance. Her philosophy is simple: "I believe virtually every problem can be solved. Mountains can be moved. It's just a matter of finding the right angle."

## Positivity

Can-do people maintain a positive attitude, even in the face of difficult challenges. Being positive is a personal choice, and people who are consistently positive tend to avoid angry, negative whiners and complainers. Positive people are too busy demonstrating the power of positive thinking. They are a source of energy that lifts up the people around them. One of the personal benefits of a positive attitude is inner happiness. Smiles come easily and naturally when we are positive.

## Purposeful

Everything in the universe has a purpose. Being aware of one's purpose is a necessary step in evolving into the best person we can be. When we know our purpose, we can align our thoughts, behaviors, and habits to be consistent with that purpose.

People who perceive themselves as spiritual beings engaged in a human experience have an advantage in discovering their mission in life. They already know that they are here for a reason, and it is just a matter of discovering their purpose.

Purpose is never about taking, getting, or acquiring more. We come into this world naked and helpless, and odds are that we will leave this world under similar conditions. Purpose is always about giving, serving, and helping in our own way to make our world a better place for our having been here.

## Principled

People who are principled have a strong sense of right and wrong. Their actions are governed by their moral and ethical beliefs. They tend to be strong, upstanding individuals who are incorruptible.

As a teenager, Steve thought he had received the call for priesthood. His high school years were spent in a seminary, but he eventually came to the conclusion that he could better serve as a social worker and therapist. He went to college and received his degrees, graduating at the time that the Vietnam War was escalating. He was immediately drafted following his graduation.

Steve believed strongly in nonviolence, and the thought of being a soldier was against his personal principles. Much to the dismay of his father, who had fought in WWII, Steve became a conscientious objector. Under tremendous family pressure, he remained true to his principles.

Many years later, Steve had a successful career as a mental health therapist and social worker. His father forgave him, finally understanding that it was not a cowardly act but a principled decision.

### Process

It is important to have goals in life. However, life is not the goal; life is living in the process. Successful people attain their goals by focusing on the everyday process of living. They live their lives in the here and now, aware of the steps and stages they experience on the way to achieving their goals.

One of the lessons of golf is to remain in the process of the swing. The goal may be to par or birdie the hole or shoot a low number for the round. When our focus shifts to the goal and away from the process, bad things begin to happen. Being conscious of the process of life is an essential ingredient in building character.

Withdrawals from the character account:

Preaching and ministering are not synonymous in my experience. Ministers are here to serve others; preachers are here to convince others to believe what they believe, and often to become wealthy in the process. Preaching is often a profitable family business handed down to subsequent generations of preachers. There have been far too many examples of religious preachers who are all talk and fail to walk the walk, resulting in public scandals and even prison terms.

Not all preachers are in the field of religion. Sometimes preaching involves urging someone else to believe or behave the way they do. I steer clear of preachers who try to tell me how to live my life. They are attempting to usurp my personal power.

The world needs people who are detail oriented. However, pettiness is an undue concern about trivial matters. There is a fine line between being detail oriented and petty. Petty people blur the line, not discerning whether a matter is important or trivial. They have difficulty seeing the bigger picture of life. Pettiness is one of my pet peeves. People of character are seldom petty.

It is amazing to me to observe a person relinquishing their personal power and becoming a victim of the world. The "poor me" approach to life is a social disease that hurts all those who come into contact with those practicing the approach.

**Questions to consider:**

Do I feel peaceful inside, regardless of what is happening outside?

Have I given away parts of my personal power?

Do I consider myself to be a positive person?

What is my grand mission or purpose for being here?

# Chapter Q

> What if our brain was designed
> To function in a quiet mind?
> Could we give up the chatter,
> As if it didn't matter,
> And leave all the noises behind?
> JB

Deposits into the character account:

## Quiet Mind

Many of us live in a noisy, stress-filled world. Urban dwellers have become accustomed to the roar of airplanes, trucks, fire engines, buses, trains, motorcycles, car traffic, police sirens, and too many people crowded into too little physical space. That amount of external stimulation can creep into our inner psyche, disquieting the mind.

I bike almost every day, often along busy streets and parkways. There can be a near-constant roar of traffic, with the periodic rumbling of a passing dump truck. It is my personal challenge to maintain a quiet mind in the midst of turmoil. I do some of my best thinking while on a bike, and I need a quiet mind in order to develop the ideas that make their way into my writings. Learning to quiet our mind in the midst of action is an important ingredient in developing character.

## Questioning

Our educational system has taught us how to think along with the crowd. It has been less effective in stimulating critical thinking. Learning to question authority figures, religious dogma, political positions, media reporting, and social customs can be an effective step in growing into our own person.

When I was growing up in Ferdinand, Indiana in the forties and fifties, asking questions was discouraged. I was expected to accept as true whatever was taught by the priests, nuns, teachers, and parents. I kept my questions to myself, knowing that some of what I was told made absolutely no sense. It wasn't until I went off to college at Indiana University that I felt free to verbalize my doubts and questions.

Nazi Germany was an excellent example of what happens to a society that is not questioning. Too many German citizens accepted Hitler's preaching, and they ultimately paid the price for going along with the crowd.

## Quality

We determine the level of quality at which we live our daily lives, the quality of the work we accomplish, and the quality of our relationships with family and friends. Some of us choose high standards of quality and demand similar standards from the other people in our lives. Some of us settle for mediocrity. A few settle for even less. Living life with high standards and expectations is an essential ingredient for building character.

Withdrawals from the character account:

*Quixotic* is a term derived from the book character Don Quixote. It can mean being impulsive, impractical, and out of touch with reality. The world needs people who are visionaries, able to imagine outside normal boundaries. When it becomes unrealistic and impractical, it can be a detriment.

People who are quick to anger tend to be defensive and difficult to deal with. When anger is the automatic response to any situation, it is a good indication that anger is the dominant emotion inside the person.

Whiners are sometimes referred to as querulous. They are often demanding, irritable, crabby, moody, and miserable. I try hard to maintain a reasonable distance from people who are querulous.

Being a quitter is sometimes appropriate if a goal is clearly out of reach or circumstances change and make continuing inappropriate. More often than not, however, quitting is an indication of lack of determination, perseverance, and/or commitment to the goal. Such quitting does not build character.

**Questions to consider:**

How do I effectively quiet my mind?

Am I willing to question authority figures or traditional thinking?

Do I expect my best effort in everything I do?

Do I persevere, or do I quit when things get tough?

# Chapter R

> What if pretenses and games
> Mask who we are deep inside?
> What if we exposed
> Our real self and supposed
> It okay to be bona fide?
> JB

Deposits into character account:

## Real

It is a challenge for many people to be who they really are. We live in a world of smoke and mirrors, where it is tempting to pretend we are someone we are not. It can be challenging to be real with ourselves and with other people.

We imagine there is something wrong with us if we think or feel a certain way. We might feel vulnerable if someone else becomes aware of our true self. We judge ourselves as flawed if we feel sad or fearful. We might even be rejected.

In order to be real, it is necessary to become mindful of what we are experiencing. Some introspection may be required to better understand the essence of our being. If we expect other people to be real with us, we better get in touch with our own real self. It is nearly impossible to connect with another person at a deep level if one is pretending.

Whenever we experience a deep, intimate connection with another human being, we can be pretty certain that both people are being real. A willingness to be vulnerable through mutual sharing generates a strong personal connection. Relationships, friendships, and character accounts are deepened as a result.

### Respectful

Respect is a possible way we treat one another and ourselves. It is an indication of admiration, esteem, or high regard. When we treat someone with respect and kindness, we tend to be treated the same way in return. When we disrespect, use derogatory names, or attack another person, it would be foolhardy to expect to be treated with respect. We receive back what we give out.

Respect means valuing another person's point of view, whether we agree with it or not. Valuing a point of view and agreeing with it are two different things. We often observe the lack of respect at the top levels of government today. Politicians are calling each other derogatory names and refusing to listen to opposing viewpoints. Respect is missing in action in parts of today's world, starting at the very top.

Rodney Dangerfield taught generations of Americans the importance of respecting ourselves. Through humor, he highlighted the consequences of a lack of self-respect. Respect is another example of being unable to give something to someone else if we don't have it ourselves.

### Relaxation

A stressful, fast-paced lifestyle can be an obstacle to being relaxed. Relaxation is a process that reduces stress on our mind and/or body. In his best-selling book *The 7 Habits of Highly Effective People*, Dr. Stephen Covey describes rest and relaxation as "sharpening the saw." Relaxation renews our personal energies to remain highly effective over the long haul.

Relaxation literally means a release of tension, resulting in less anger, anxiety, or fear. An entire industry has been created to teach relaxation techniques to highly stressed individuals. Learning to relax is an important lesson for building character.

## Reliability

A reliable person can be depended on to do the job. They are trustworthy because they have a track record of performing consistently well. Reliability is an important character trait for anyone to have but particularly for a partner, employee, coworker, or friend. We all try to surround ourselves with reliable people.

As a sole practitioner for many years, I was the only person I could depend on to get the job done. After a decade in solo practice, I hired Tracy to be a second attorney in my firm. A primary reason I hired her was that she exuded reliability and dependability. I sensed that she was trustworthy, and I was not disappointed. As I slowly eased my way out of the practice and into retirement, Tracy assumed more and more responsibility. Eventually I felt comfortable to retire from the practice of law, knowing that our clients were in capable, dependable hands. Tracy had developed the depth of character required for the job.

## Reasonableness

Most people are rational and reasonable much of the time. It is difficult to relate to a person who lacks the ability or the willingness to be sensible, fair-minded, equitable, or even sane. I am convinced that many politicians in Washington, DC, have knowingly abandoned reasonableness in exchange for special interest groups, their voting base, and raising money to finance future campaigns. Those politicians have closed out their character accounts.

Withdrawals from the character account:

Revenge involves intentionally and maliciously inflicting hurt on someone who has been perceived as treating us with less respect than we think we deserve. It is a desire to repay an injury with an injury. Being a revengeful person is not an effective way to build character. Revenge can lead to long-running feuds, fist fights, duels, and even wars. Revenge has reared its ugly head recently at the highest levels of American government.

There is never an acceptable excuse for being rude. It means being impolite, ill mannered, and nasty. Rudeness has no place in a civilized society. A person who is acting rude may as well carry a sign saying, "I am stupid!" It is a behavior with its origins in fear. Rudeness destroys character.

Being a racist or bigot in today's world demonstrates an extremely low level of functioning. After all the social messages to the contrary, people who still hold on to their racist tendencies are simply acting from fear. Fear is an enemy of character.

## Questions to consider:

Do I try to mask or deny who I really am deep inside?

How do I treat other people in my life? Do I consistently honor and respect them?

What are my favorite ways to relax and regenerate?

Do I harbor racist tendencies toward any group of people?

# Chapter S

*What if inner strength
Is the fuel that leads to success?
It allows us to go to great lengths
In an effort to be our best.*
JB

Deposits into the character account:

## STRENGTH

Physical strength can be an asset in our journey through life, but it pales in comparison to the importance of strength of mind. Inner strength means having the mental and emotional skills, resources, and determination to deal with difficult challenges. It means not giving up in the face of adversity. It means hanging tough.

Just as developing physical fitness and strength is an ongoing process, building inner strength can be a lifelong exercise. Regardless of body type, anyone can choose to transform themselves into a tough, powerful person inside. Some of the ingredients of strength of mind can include a physical fitness program that provides the energy necessary to develop inner strength; being active and proactive, rather than sitting around waiting for something to change; being surrounded by positive people, who can help to maintain a positive attitude; being introspective and taking a longer view of life; being open to divine guidance through prayer and meditation; and resisting the urge for self-pity and feeling powerless.

One thing we know about life is that we will be faced with difficult challenges from time to time. The challenge may be in the form of a serious illness, the death of a loved one, financial setbacks, business failures, unwanted divorce, being disappointed by a loved one, or all the above. The key to a life well lived is not whether we have challenges but rather how we respond when challenged. Developing inner strength is a giant step toward character building.

## Sincerity

It feels natural to associate with sincere individuals. There is a sense of security when the person we are with is open, truthful, and straightforward. We know where we stand and do not worry about the person being dishonest, deceptive, misleading, or hypocritical. There is a genuineness that goes along with sincerity.

A sincere politician has become a rarity. Too many political figures make it a game about winning and getting reelected, rather than making a sincere effort to do what is truly helpful. That is a major reason why so many current politicians are held in such low regard by the electorate.

## Service

At his inaugural address, John F. Kennedy made a profound statement about serving that left an impression on me as an eighteen-year-old, and it remains with me more than half a century later: "My fellow Americans, ask not what your country can do for you; ask what you can do for your country."

The philosophy of service is strong in many aspects of American life. Many members of our military are motivated to serve; most law enforcement officials, firefighters, schoolteachers, nurses, and doctors are dedicated to serving the public. Some political office holders and government workers are focused on service, and many workers in service industries take their responsibilities very seriously.

When professionals and businesses have a mission to serve, rather than a simple goal to make as much money as possible, they tend to succeed in the long run. Just as giving and receiving are the same, service to others usually results in the success of the server. It comes full circle.

## Serenity

Nearly everyone knows the opening verse of the Serenity Prayer: "God, grant me the serenity to accept the things I cannot change, courage to change the things I can, and wisdom to know the difference." Serenity means a state of mind that is calm and peaceful. It is a blissful state that is conducive to being effective and productive, untroubled by distractions or irritations. Being serene is an excellent building block for character building.

## Security

We know people who appear to be secure in their own skin. They exude an aura of confidence, unafraid of any challenge that life may throw their way. It is a calming effect to be in the company of a person who is genuinely secure.

Being secure is often a learned trait, following years of life experiences, including successes and failures. True security comes from understanding that we are spiritual beings engaged in a human life experience.

## Sanity

Being sane merely means having a healthy mind that is able to think and behave in a normal and rational manner. Some people have the ability to be perfectly sane in most areas of their lives but become unhinged in others. The inability of a political leader to demonstrate sanity when questioned or criticized is an unsettling thing. Thinking and acting sanely in all aspects of our life is a way to build our character account.

## Sharing

There are many ways to share that can help to build character. Being willing to share our thoughts and feelings openly and freely can be an important ingredient in relationships, whether the sharing is with a spouse, partner, or friend. Sharing in our abundance with those less fortunate is another way to build character.

Withdrawals from the character account:

Sarcasm has a strong presence in our society, and it is not a helpful quality. Sarcastic people think it is acceptable to use irony (sometimes in the name of humor) to mock or ridicule another person. It can be a cruel way to convey contempt. Sarcasm does not represent a high level of communication, and it can be damaging and hurtful. People of character are not sarcastic.

A person who is shameless has no sense of decency. Such a person is willing to be flagrantly dishonest or outrageous, seemingly insensible to disgrace. Shamelessness and good conscience are mutually exclusive.

Selfishness is the flip side of sharing. When we are interested only in our own personal profit, gain, or pleasure, we disconnect ourselves from the rest of the world. Character is generally not built in isolation.

Self-centeredness is an egotistical attitude that can reach to narcissism, which is a form of mental illness. Self-centered people are selfish, having no regard for the rest of the world. It is all about them.

Shyness is often associated with a lack of self-confidence. It is the tendency to feel awkward or tense about social engagements. Shyness is usually rooted in fear of rejection or discomfort in connecting with other people. Shyness can be an obstacle to character development. Overcoming shyness can be a liberating step along the way to growing character.

**Questions to consider:**

How well do I deal with difficult challenges?

Would I rather serve or be served?

How willing am I to share my true thoughts and feelings with people close to me?

Is a sense of shyness holding me back from evolving into the person I want to be?

# Chapter T

*What if our thoughts*
*Determine our fate,*
*From success to doubts,*
*From loving to hate?*
JB

Deposits into the character account:

## Trust

When we trust another person, we have faith and confidence that the person is capable and honest. When we trust ourselves, it means that we have confidence in our own ability to succeed. Trust is a necessary ingredient in quality relationships, and it is also necessary for our own self-esteem.

Some people have an innate sense of being trustworthy. It exudes from the essence of their being. Others have to work to earn trust. Either way, it is a key ingredient for a person of character. Not everyone develops a reputation for being worthy of trust.

I have practiced law for most of my adult life. The legal profession offers a wide-ranging spectrum of trustworthiness.

A small segment of the bar (all of whom will remain nameless) was commonly regarded by their fellow attorneys as shady characters that could not be trusted. These attorneys might say anything or do anything to get desirable results. They were not trusted by judges, fellow lawyers, or clients. On the other end of the spectrum, a significant portion of the bar was considered eminently trustworthy. They consistently did the right thing, and their word was their bond.

## Tolerance

Tolerant people have the ability, and are willing, to accept different opinions, behaviors, or appearances. They are fair and objective about others' beliefs, practices, religious background, and racial or ethnic origins. In other words, tolerant people are not judgmental, bigoted, or hateful.

I grew up in a small town that did not value tolerance. In the fifties, it seemed like everyone was expected to believe and act in certain ways. Anyone who was different was not accepted. Nonwhites and non-Catholics were not welcomed with open arms. Anyone questioning the conventional wisdom was shunned. It was an environment based on ignorance and fear. Tolerance, on the other hand, is based on enlightenment and loving one another. It leads to character building.

## Toughness

The word *tough* has multiple meanings. What I mean is that a tough person has the strength and determination to withstand difficult situations. Tough people endure hardships and difficulties and come out stronger for the experience.

An old friend, Don, lost his job and was diagnosed with a brain tumor the same week. To make matters worse, he was married with four small children and his marriage was crumbling. Many people in his situation would have given up. Don somehow found an inner grace and toughness that enabled him to persevere through his difficulties. He went on to become the director of the Center for Attitudinal Healing in Sausalito, sharing his own experience and demonstrating the possibilities when we choose love over fear and peace over conflict. Don recently published a book entitled *The End of Stress* that provides a step-by-step approach to mastering stress in our lives.

## Thoughtful

Considerate, caring friends are valuable treasures. Thoughtful people are able to pay attention to the needs of others, demonstrating concern, understanding, and compassion. They tend to be good listeners, observant, and helpful. Thoughtful individuals usually have loads of character.

## Thankful

Feeling thankful is a choice, a personal decision. We can appreciate and be grateful for the circumstances in our lives, or we can be totally oblivious of our many blessings. One person may be thankful for the same thing that another person angrily resents.

Cultivating a personal consciousness of gratitude can make a tremendous difference in the quality of our lives. Thankful people tend to be happy people. They develop a deep appreciation for each day.

## Tenacity

To be tenacious is to be determined, persevering regardless of obstacles or challenges along the way. Tenacity requires a strong sense of purpose, patience, and endurance.

Marathon runners are tenacious, refusing to quit running when the body is running out of energy. A college student requires tenacity during the semester's final week of exams. A worker needs tenacity when a deadline looms for a big project. Tenacity makes us stronger and builds character.

Withdrawals from the character account:

Business and politics seem to generate toady people who pander, flatter, and suck up to powerful people in order to win their favor. They grovel in order to ingratiate themselves to the boss, often putting down others in order to climb over them. Washington, DC, is populated with toady personalities. A toady has no depth or strength of character.

When we are thin-skinned, we are overly sensitive to criticism. Thin-skinned people are easily offended and defensive. Sadly, they are not able to learn from constructive criticism because they take the criticism personally. Most of us are thin-skinned from time to time and try hard to overcome it. It is particularly damaging to have a defensive, thin-skinned person at the head of a business or government.

A toxic personality can cause tremendous social problems. Like a dangerous chemical, spewing poisonous thoughts and words into business or social situations can cause long-term damage. The toxic personality is angry, unhappy, and misguided. It can bankrupt a character account.

People who focus on taking rather than giving are some of the saddest people in the world. Takers can never get enough of anything and blame other people for not giving them what they want or need. Living a life based on taking is a lonely, sad way to live.

Being tedious can be a sure way to be perceived as too slow, dull, boring, and monotonous. Tedious behavior can be carrying thoroughness to an extreme. Some jobs are necessarily tedious, such as working on an assembly line, performing brain surgery, or repairing watches, but most jobs are not.

**Questions to consider:**

Who are the people in my life that I most trust?

What is my level of trust and confidence in me?

Do I remember to be thankful every day?

Am I tenacious enough and tough enough to accomplish my goals?

# Chapter U

> What if good intentions
> Are sometimes misunderstood,
> Becoming the cause of dissension
> Instead of intending for good?
> JB

Deposits into the character account:

## Understanding

There are happenings in this world that are beyond understanding. Mass shootings, terrorist attacks, and gratuitous violence can stretch our ability to grasp the meaning of the actions. On the other hand, making an effort to understand one another, being open to varying perspectives, and being kind to everyone can impact the amount of unreasonable behavior in the world.

Misunderstandings are a great source of unnecessary conflict. Understanding requires a willingness to listen and a tendency not to judge. Understandings among diverse points of view require an openness that is rare in our society. Too often there is a rush to judgment with an expectation for the worst.

When we are in the presence of a kind, understanding person, it is easy to sense the peaceful power of that person. Art was a highly respected senior partner in a Northern Indiana law firm. It is not uncommon for attorneys to become overzealous in the representation of their clients in adversarial matters. I was in awe of Art's ability to insert himself into the battle and calmly get the warring parties to discuss their real needs and concerns. He had a knack for grasping the true issues lying beneath the rhetoric, defusing powder kegs, and bringing the parties together to find a mutually satisfactory result. Art's character was obvious.

## Unity

We live in a society that promotes separation. We are separated by religious beliefs; differences in political philosophies; and wealth, education, race, gender, and ethnicity. Beneath the differences, however, there is a quality of oneness that has the potential to bring us together. Beyond our humanness, we share a common bond. The same life force courses through every one of us. Our spirits are all connected. To the extent that we can learn to channel our individual talents for the greater good, our society will live either in harmony or in disharmony.

We have a surplus of political and religious leaders who push in the direction of separation. We desperately need more leadership directed toward unification, common interests, and spiritual ideals.

## Uplifting

There are people among us who have the power and commitment to uplift, moving us to a higher place, a higher level of functioning. Some religious leaders have assumed this role, inspiring congregants to become the best persons they can be. Pope Francis is setting such an example on a worldwide basis, challenging Catholics and other faiths to step up to a higher level. Dr. Martin Luther King Jr. fought nonviolently for racial equality and a better world. John F. Kennedy was a political leader who taught an entire nation to aim higher, to not be satisfied with mediocrity. Every one of these leaders was a person of character. I believe we have barely scratched the surface when it comes to functioning at higher levels. Education and leadership are the keys to uplifting our entire society.

## Unafraid

Fear is perhaps the greatest obstacle to a life well lived; we must be unafraid. It shows up in life in a myriad of ways that ultimately limit our personal power. As I wrote in *The Bike Writer*, fear can manifest as shyness, stress, worry, depression, insecurity, anger, arrogance, defensiveness, selfishness, bigotry, greed, discrimination, bullying, and a general unwillingness to explore new adventures. Overcoming fear can be a difficult process for those of us who were raised in a fearful environment. It is, however, absolutely essential that we learn to live without fear if we want a happy, fulfilling life that is filled with character.

## Unpretentious

Society seems to promote the concept of exaggerating our self-importance, talents, and wealth in order to impress someone else. Pretentious people pretend they are more important than the rest of us. It can come out as ostentatious displays of wealth, entitlement to special treatment in restaurants, or snobbish behavior that demonstrates feelings of superiority.

In my estate-planning law practice, I got to know clients who had been highly successful in business, accumulating much wealth, and had legitimate reasons to feel important. I most admired the ones who remained unpretentious, enjoying and sharing their wealth with the less fortunate and quietly using their resources to make a positive difference in the world. They were the ones with an abundance of character.

## Unbiased

Being unbiased is not always an easy task. Every person has had different family, education, culture, and life experiences. We all bring our highly developed filters into any situation. The truly unbiased individual is a rarity. Unbiased means total freedom from all prejudice or favoritism. These are the people who exude character.
Withdrawals from the character account:

Ugliness has a much deeper meaning than physical appearance. It refers to behaving in an unpleasant, repulsive manner. Ugly behavior is another trait rooted in fear. It is a way for an insecure person to get noticed. Acting in an ugly fashion is a cry for help.

Unethical people lack moral principles. They fail to conform to appropriate moral standards. Being an unethical professional can be cause for losing the license to practice a profession. Being unethical is never acceptable for a highly functioning person.

I have known a few uppity people in my lifetime, and I could not distance myself from them fast enough. An uppity person tends to be arrogant, snobbish, and overbearing, with a general feeling of superiority over the masses. Being uppity does not build character.

## Questions to consider:

Who is the person in my life who is the most understanding? What can I learn from that person?

Am I functioning at a level that reflects my true potential?

Do I consider myself different from or better than other people?

# Chapter V

> What if victory is fleeting,
> If winning involves cheating?
> What if veracity counts,
> Whether in a losing effort or trounce?
> JB

Deposits into the character account:

# Values

Our values largely determine how we conduct our daily lives. Values are the ongoing beliefs and ideals for the culture or society we call home. They influence our attitudes and behavior, guiding us as we move through life.

If our culture values violence, it is likely that our actions will be governed by our violent urges. If peace is a predominant value, we will probably act and react in peaceful ways. If honesty and truthfulness are treasured values, our conduct will probably be consistently honest. If lying and cheating is the acceptable norm, that is the course we will tend to follow.

Notwithstanding the values espoused by the environment we are in, we are free to choose the values that make sense to us. If we find ourselves in uncomfortable situations, we can choose to break out of the cultural norms and change our values and our conduct. We do not have to be victims of our world.

Sometimes it takes the influence of one person—perhaps a parent or teacher—to help a child break free of a negative environment with poor values. Zach grew up in the middle of a big city, with gang violence the order of the day. Zach's father was in prison for dealing drugs, and Zach's mother was raising him alone, while working two jobs to make ends meet. She sacrificed her life to give Zach a chance to break out of the violent, dangerous atmosphere of their neighborhood. She instilled in Zach the values of honesty, integrity, kindness, and hard work. She enrolled him in a special school where he could excel with his musical talents. Today Zach is a professional musician who helps children with backgrounds similar to his own, guiding and mentoring them in a higher set of values.

## Veracity

In this era of "fake news" and "alternative facts," veracity has taken on an even more important meaning. The accuracy and correctness of political comments are no longer trustworthy; media reports may or may not be truthful; social media messaging is not always what it purports to be; business and banking practices may be misleading or downright corrupt. Bias and profit have often taken precedence over veracity.

As individuals we have a choice. Do we follow those leaders who are driven by winning at any cost? Or do we choose to conform to the truth and act with integrity and honesty? Our character depends on the choices we make.

## Valor

*Valor* is often defined as bravery on the battle field. It is that and more. Valor means honor and dignity in the face of danger or difficulty. It requires strength of mind, spirit, and character to encounter danger with boldness and bravery.

Heroes and heroines come in all shapes, sizes, colors, and religious backgrounds. They arise from doing the right thing, no matter how difficult it may be. Valor is a valued trait for soldiers, firefighters, law enforcement officers, doctors, nurses, teachers, politicians, business executives, and ministers. Not every person of character includes valor as a trait. It is like the icing on the cake.

## Vibrancy

People who are vibrant add energy and spirit to every situation, making life more passionate, intense, and interesting. They seem to sparkle in the midst of mediocrity. We are naturally drawn to vibrant people who remind us of what is possible. They bring living color to an otherwise colorless world.

Withdrawals from the character account:

Vain people have excessive admiration for their own appearance or ability. Vanity goes far beyond self-esteem, bordering on egotism and narcissism. The term applies to conceited people who have a foolish belief in their own value. Vanity is not a building block of character.

There are real victims who are harmed, injured, or even killed as a result of crime, disease, or accident. Unfortunately, there are also victims of the world who live their lives with a "poor me" attitude. They feel cheated by God, parents, siblings, teachers, or employers. These victims are quick to blame, without accepting any responsibility for their predicament.

Often victims of the world are vengeful. They can be vindictive, unforgiving, always seeking to avenge a perceived slight. People focused on revenge tend to lead sad, angry, unfulfilling lives.

Vicious people are deliberately cruel, intentionally hurting or harming someone else. Vicious behavior often leads to additional forms of damage and can come full circle back to hurting the offending person. Vicious people lack character.

**Questions to consider:**

How do I define my core values?

How do I personally react to misleading, untruthful messages?

Do I ever feel like a victim? If so, what kinds of situations cause me to feel like a victim?

Have I ever intentionally hurt another person?

# CHAPTER W

What if all wisdom and knowledge
Is not acquired while in college,
If we remain open-minded
And refuse to be blinded
To the wisdom and knowledge of colleagues?
JB

Deposits into the character account:

## WISDOM

Wise people may or may not be smart. Wisdom is the integration of knowledge and experience in a way that provides a deep understanding. It involves common sense, insights, and good judgment. Wisdom is acquired through interactions with other people, introspection, and an open mind.

Jack was not a good student in school. He counted the days until he graduated from high school and never even considered going to college. Jack probably had a learning disability, but learning disabilities were not part of the vocabulary in his small town so many years ago.

Although poorly educated, Jack had innate knowledge of how the world worked. His military experience opened him up to other cultures and other parts of the world. He developed strong relationships and was a good friend to many. People liked to hang around with Jack, enjoying his sense of humor and listening to his stories.

Jack, with his wife, raised a family of four children. He instilled in his children a work ethic and an ability to have fun and enjoy life at the same time. In times of trouble, Jack could be counted on to provide an insight and astuteness that far exceeded his educational background. His wisdom came from the school of hard knocks. Jack was a character with character, and he is sorely missed by friends and family.

## Warmth

Warmth has a multitude of meanings. Human warmth is a quality that includes genuineness, kindness, enthusiasm, and affection. Everyone wants to be around warm personalities. We feel loved in the presence of human warmth.

As a child, I remember my dad as the parent with the most warmth. Mom was more cautious, reserved, and responsible. Dad, on the other hand, had the innate ability to convey a sense of playfulness, tenderness, caring, and affection for everyone, including his children. His playful sense of humor was present even under trying circumstances. He genuinely liked and enjoyed people, and people in turn genuinely liked and enjoyed him.

## Wholeness

Wholeness means being a complete person—physically, mentally, emotionally, and spiritually. It is integration and balancing of body, mind, and spirit. It means living life with a high level of energy and integrity.

Wholeness is not an easy condition to achieve on a consistent basis. The people I know who demonstrate wholeness eat healthy, exercise often, and manage their stress levels through stress-reduction techniques, prayer, and meditation. Wholeness is a ticket to character.

## Work Ethic

A strong work ethic is essential for a business to succeed. It is also an essential quality for personal success. Work ethic involves a set of moral principles that guide behavior at work. It means being self-motivated and consistently producing high-quality work.

People with a good work ethic are dedicated to the job at hand, whether it is being a CEO or a janitor, a teacher or a student, a parent or spouse. They tend to be cooperative, productive, and self-disciplined. Having a good work ethic and having character are consistent qualities.

## Welcoming

We are drawn to those people and organizations that extend a friendly welcome and make the effort for others to feel comfortable in their presence. They seem genuinely glad to bring us into their spheres. They appreciate having other people in their lives, whether the others are family members, friends, strangers, or people of different religions, colors, and ethnicities. Welcoming people and organizations tend to be nonjudgmental, open, tolerant, and fair. These are all key ingredients in building character.

Withdrawals from the character account:

Whining is a disease that weakens character. Normal people try their best to avoid whiners. There is no joy when whining is present in the room. According to James Allen, in his classic book *As a Man Thinketh*, "A man only begins to be a man when he ceases to whine, and commences to search for the hidden justice which regulates his life." Whining and character are mutually exclusive.

Being wasteful seems to be a uniquely American characteristic. Many of us waste food, fuel, energy, and resources. Most other countries do not have the luxury of being wasteful. Wasting precious resources is not a character builder.

We all know people who seem to be on the warpath much of the time, wreaking their wrath on anyone unfortunate enough to cross their paths. Living a life filled with wrath is not an effective way to build character.

Someone who is wishy-washy is seen as feeble, weak, indecisive, and ineffectual. They lack the boldness and strength of character to be strong, vibrant members of society.

## Questions to consider:

Who are the wisest people in my life?

Do I exude warmth to other people? If not, what is holding me back?

Am I a welcoming person?

Do I think of myself as strong and decisive or wishy-washy?

# Chapter X

> What if we looked past the external
> To the person deep inside?
> Could we see the spirit eternal
> That within the body resides?
> JB

Deposits into the character account:

## X-Ray Vision

If Superman can have x-ray vision, it seems to me that it should be available to everyone. In the context of character building, being able to see beyond physical appearances is vital. We are not our bodies, the clothes we wear, the vehicles we drive, or the homes we live in. The essence of our being goes way beyond those physical elements.

When we judge another person based on appearances, we fail to see the real person. We are focused on the frame rather than the artwork within the frame. We are missing the point of life. Appearances may or may not reflect the person inside. The person inside is developed and nurtured through a lifetime of experiences, personal choices, inner thoughts, relationships with others, cultural values, and behaviors. Contrary to popular opinion, clothes do not make the person.

Likewise, when we look on the American flag as America, we are confusing the symbol of America with the inner essence of America. America at its best is freedom loving, tolerant, fair, helpful, service oriented, generous, and kind. That is the America I choose to know: a nation of welcoming, strong, open-minded people who have character, regardless of their religious beliefs, race, ethnicity, color, or style of dress.

America is made up of people who are free to speak out and express their thoughts and feelings. The true American consistently does the right thing, and sometimes the right thing may not be the popular thing to do. The right thing may be to abolish the slavery system. The right thing may be to stand up to a dictatorship that is threatening another part of the world. The right thing may be to speak out against injustice in the system. That consistent willingness to do the right thing over the centuries has made America the great nation that it is. The flag is the symbolic icing on the cake.

Withdrawals from the character account:

Xenophobia is the irrational, deep-rooted fear or hatred of strangers, especially strangers from foreign countries or different cultures. Historically, America is the melting pot for people from every nation and culture in the world. This diversity has provided great strength and prosperity over the centuries. Xenophobia appears to be on the rise in the twenty-first century. Xenophobes are making large withdrawals from America's collective character account.

## Questions to consider:

When I meet a stranger, what do I see?

How much do I value all the freedoms guaranteed by the United States Constitution?

Am I afraid of people who look different from me?

## Chapter Y

> What if the best
> Is yet to come?
> What if life's test
> Has just begun?
> JB

Deposits into the character account:

## Yet

Regardless of age or physical condition, we can develop the attitude that the best in life is yet to come. Maintaining a positive attitude is a cornerstone to a life well lived. The future is created from our present thoughts and attitudes.

We have all known people who have given up on life. They feel that their lives are over once they reach a certain stage in life, face a health challenge, or lose a spouse or friend. If that is what they think, they are probably right. But we also know people who accept the challenge, plan for a better future, and continue to enjoy all that life has to offer.

Jerry was devastated when his wife died after a marriage that spanned almost half a century. They had shared lives well lived. After Sophie died, Jerry went through several years of mourning and depression. He lost the sense of humor, which had been his hallmark for all the years that I had known him. I thought Jerry was on his way out of life, but he surprised me.

Through his volunteer activities, Jerry met Ann, whose husband had died a few years before. When they came to my office for estate-planning purposes, I barely recognized Jerry. His lively energy and sense of humor had returned and multiplied. He was the "old Jerry," only better. They went on to have many happy years together. For Jerry the best was yet to come. He was a character with character.

### Yes

Certain people seem to have the innate attitude of "Yes, I can." They have the self-confidence and willingness to do whatever is required to accomplish a task, develop a concept, or succeed in business. I believe this is an attitude that can also be developed over time, whether or not it is our natural inclination.

Success tends to build on success. The more consistently we accept the challenge, the easier it gets to accomplish great things. For some of us, it is an acquired talent based on hard work and effort. The doers of the world are priceless treasures that benefit everyone.

### Yoga

There are disciplines and practices that tend to be conducive to improving our lives. Yoga is one such discipline. Originating in India centuries ago, yoga is a combination of physical, mental, and spiritual disciplines that have spread across the world. Its popularity in the Western world is a testament to the personal benefits available from this ancient practice. It can enhance character.

Withdrawals from the character account:

Opposed to the attitude of "Yes, I can," there is an attitude of being a yes-man. This is the kind of person who agrees with the boss or authority figure, whether or not they truly agree. This person is constantly attempting to gain approval, even if it sacrifices their principles. We see yes-men in the business world, the political sphere, and family life. These toadies lack a mental or emotional spine and willingly give up their character accounts.

## Questions to consider:

Do I sometimes feel that the best parts of my life are in the past?

Am I a competent person who can accomplish anything I set my mind to?

Do I stand up for my principles when a boss figure suggests otherwise?

# Chapter Z

*What if all fears*
*Are just in my mind?*
*When my mind clears,*
*Inner peace do I find.*
JB

Deposits into the character account:

## Zero Fears

At Franklin D. Roosevelt's first inaugural address, America was in the grips of the Great Depression. His famous "There is nothing to fear but fear itself" statement was key to the recovery of an entire nation from the terror that had paralyzed the United States and world economies. Living in fear is one of the saddest conditions of humankind; we should strive to have zero fears. Fearful people are frequently unable to function up to their potential. Individuals and cultures living in a fearful state of mind give up their power to succeed in life. The condition can be contagious, as it appears to be in North Korea. A fear-based mind is a barrier to joy, inner peace, or love. Fear is an ego-based emotion.

We are free to choose the thoughts that create our mindset. At least in America, fearful thoughts are a choice, and they can be overcome and replaced by confident, positive thoughts. The greatest obstacle to success is fear of failure. Books have been written and psychological and motivational techniques have been developed to help people through the process of overcoming a fearful mind.

## Zeal

People with zeal are energized, motivated, and willing to pursue their dreams. They have an enthusiasm and passion for life. It can be infectious. Being around a person with zeal tends to activate and energize everyone else. People with zeal tend to ascend to leadership positions in organizations. There is an aura about them that causes other people to admire and respect them.

## Zen

Zen thinking, derived from Buddhism, is an approach that seeks religious enlightenment through meditation in which there is no consciousness of self. The practice helps the person to relax and not worry about things beyond his or her control. It can also help to build character.

Withdrawals from the character account:

Living zonked out or unconscious from alcohol or narcotic drugs is a sure way to waste a precious life. Being stoned may lead to being a character, but it is not an effective way to build character.

## Questions to consider:

What fears have I overcome so far in my life?

What are the fears that remain for me to conquer?

How have my fears held me back from my goals?

# CLOSING THOUGHTS

### Just Passing Through

All the billions of people on earth right now are my fellow travelers on this human journey. Most of them bear little physical resemblance to me. Some of them have a different skin color, and they live in quite different cultures and lead different lifestyles from my own. We travel different paths using different vehicles to cross different terrains. Beneath the surface, however, we are eerily similar. The bottom line is that we are all just passing through this human experience.

If this life is indeed a human journey, let's not turn it into a guilt trip or an ego trip. Unless reincarnation is the reality of humanity, this may be our one chance to travel this path. It deserves our best shot of us functioning at our highest potential.

### Reflections on Seventy-Five Years

Three-quarters of a century have passed since I began my journey in Ferdinand, Indiana, in the middle years of WWII. Just two days before my birth, more than ninety thousand German troops surrendered to the Soviets at Stalingrad. Many more thousands of German and Soviet troops failed to survive this pivotal battle on the eastern front, and I sometimes wonder if my nonviolent tendencies are the result of the spirit of a slain soldier entering my physical body at the time of my birth.

From Ferdinand to Bloomington (Indiana University) to Indianapolis (law school) to Fort Wayne to Bonita Springs, it has been an interesting, challenging, rewarding, and humbling trip. I can hardly wait to find out what lies ahead on the journey.

There have been major forks in the road, which have required choices like giving up basketball at age sixteen to work as a warehouse boy after school, letting go of my dream of being a journalist and writer in favor of economics and law school, recovering from an early overdose of Catholicism, ending a twenty-year marriage that wasn't working the way we had planned, committing to a second-chance marriage with Jan, leaving an established law firm to practice law my way, retiring from the practice of law following heart surgery, making biking my vehicle for rehabilitation from bypass surgery, helping Jan to build a real estate business in Florida, and coming full circle to becoming a writer in my seventies.

There have been unexpected detours that have required patience. There have been bumps in the road that have been painful. I've gotten lost a few times. Through it all, I've learned about life. I wouldn't change a thing, even if I could. More than anything, I view life as a learning experience.

## Leaving a Legacy

Twenty or fifty or one hundred years from now, no trace of our physical presence will remain. We began this journey with nothing, and no matter how much stuff we accumulate while we are here, we will leave with nothing. Our investments, bank accounts, homes, and physical possessions will have been liquidated and dispersed or transferred in kind to future generations.

Like a dog on a walk, we will leave markers along the path that will be our legacy. We will be remembered or quickly forgotten by future generations based on the way we conduct our lives while we are here.

Some of us will leave behind businesses or charitable organizations that we helped to establish or grow. Some of us will leave books or songs or paintings that we have created that will be around long after we are gone. My mother left behind a handmade quilt for each one of her thirty grandchildren.

Personally, I would like to be remembered, at least for a while, as someone who spent his time wisely, making the world a better place for having been here. I want to be remembered as a person of character.

**What will be your legacy?**

What are the things that have happened so far that you feel really good about?

What are your biggest accomplishments?

What are the obstacles you have overcome?

What are your greatest lessons?

Where do you go from here?

How will you be remembered?

# POWERFUL AFFIRMATIONS FOR CHARACTER BUILDING

Many people engage in negative self-talk on a daily basis, which can ultimately convince us that we are ugly, stupid, or born losers. The antidote to negative self-talk is a daily dose of positive affirmations that boost self-esteem and literally transform the way we view ourselves.

In my experience, affirmations are most effective when repeated in the first, second, and third person: "I, (name), am strong, confident, secure; you, (name), are strong, confident, secure; he/she, (name), is strong, confident, secure." Affirmations can be in writing or quietly said to ourselves as we meditate, walk, or bike. Below are some examples of affirmations.

- I, _____, am evolving, growing, learning to be the best person I can be.
- I, _____, am calm, relaxed, peaceful inside.
- I, _____, am strong, confident, unafraid.
- I, _____, am happy, content, blessed.
- I, _____, am healthy, strong, fit.
- I, _____, am a warm, friendly, caring friend.

# ABOUT THE AUTHOR

Jim Boeglin is a retired attorney who lives with his wife, Jan, in Bonita Springs, Florida. Between the two of them, they have three children and four grandchildren. Two years after leaving Fort Wayne, Indiana, for retirement in Florida, they both became licensed Realtors and formed the Boeglin Team.

In his seventies, Jim began to pursue his lifelong dream of writing books. His first book, *The Bike Writer*, discussed insights discovered along the bicycle paths of life. The book received rave reviews from family members and friends. Jim is hoping for a wider audience for *Character Building*.

CPSIA information can be obtained
at www.ICGtesting.com
Printed in the USA
LVOW11s1231100618
580227LV00001B/53/P

9 781480 862135